STRENGTHEN YOUR MARRIAGE, GROW IN FAITH

A Workbook for Couples to Grow Spiritually and Deepen Intimacy

DAQUAN N. MOSES

DISCLAIMER

The information provided in this workbook is intended for educational and informational purposes only, to assist couples in strengthening their marriage and growing in their faith. It is not intended as a substitute for professional advice from a licensed therapist, counselor, or other qualified relationship specialist.

Specifically, any financial advice provided in this workbook is for informational purposes only and should not be considered a substitute for professional financial advice. If you need financial guidance, please consult with a qualified financial advisor.

While the exercises and guidance in this workbook can be helpful for improving communication, resolving conflict, and deepening intimacy in your marriage, they are not intended to diagnose or treat any specific marital or relational challenges.

If you are experiencing significant challenges in your marriage or have concerns about your relationship, please seek professional help from a qualified specialist.

The author and publisher are not responsible for any adverse effects or consequences resulting from the use of this workbook.

Thank you for choosing this workbook! I am excited that you are taking this step towards strengthening your marriage and growing in your faith together.

Your willingness to invest in your relationship and prioritize your spiritual connection is an inspiration. I believe that by actively engaging with the exercises and reflections in this workbook, you can deepen your communication, resolve conflict constructively, and build a more intimate and fulfilling marriage.

Remember, marriage is a lifelong adventure that requires constant learning, growing, and relying on God's guidance. This workbook is your companion on this journey, providing you with biblical principles and practical tools to create a God-centered marriage that thrives.

I appreciate your trust in me and wish you all the best on your journey towards a stronger marriage and a deeper faith.

With warm regards,

Daquan N. Moses.

This workbook belongs to

____

____

Dedication

To couples who dare to dream of a love that grows stronger each year, a faith that keeps them together in the face of adversity, and an extraordinary connection.

May this workbook be a compass and companion as you attempt to create a marriage that exemplifies Christ's enduring love.

Acknowledgement

This workbook would not exist without the numerous conversations with couples who generously shared their struggles and successes. Their candor lit these pages, their perseverance inspired the exercises, and their commitment to growth formed the foundation of this work.

I want to give a special thanks to my friends and coworkers, who provided invaluable feedback, questioned my assumptions, and encouraged me during the long hours of writing and revising. Your support kept the momentum going.

Finally, my spouse's love is an ongoing source of strength and support. Thank you for believing in our endeavor and constantly reminding me of the beauty and power of a strong marriage.

Above all, we thank God for his grace, love, and wisdom as we begin this lifelong journey of marriage. May this workbook serve as a testament to His faithfulness and a tool for strengthening the holy bond of marriage.

Why This Workbook?

A successful marriage doesn't just happen, it necessitates intention, commitment, and a desire to grow, both personally and collectively.

This workbook provides resources and directions for:

- Deepen your connection: Move beyond surface-level encounters and allow for actual intimacy.

- Improve your communication skills: Learn to actively listen and express yourself honestly, even when things are challenging.

- Constructive conflict resolution is honing the ability to navigate confrontations with dignity and understanding.

- Develop your faith as a marriage by praying together, studying Scripture, and establishing a shared spiritual foundation.

- Create a shared vision: Discuss your long-term goals and encourage one another.

This is more than simply another marriage book. It is an invitation to actively participate in shaping a marriage that honors and reflects God's love.

Introduction

A healthy Christian marriage exudes love, joy, and perseverance, demonstrating the strength of shared faith and dedication. It's a partnership in which two people, united by their love for one another and their devotion to God, face life's challenges together, their ties strengthened by each triumph and storm they endure. Such a marriage is an ongoing journey of growth, discovery, and greater connection. It's a dance between two spirits, choreographed by grace and guided by the steady light of trust.

This workbook encourages you to follow that road and actively participate in building a marriage that honors God and shows His love. It is a toolkit for couples seeking a deeper, more rewarding relationship, as well as a road map for those hoping to strengthen their bond and leave a lasting legacy of love. These sections feature useful advice, engaging tasks, and thought-provoking questions designed to spark meaningful conversations and inspire thoughtful action.

At its core, this workbook explores the delicate dance of improving your marriage and growing in religion. It recognizes that these two pursuits are not separate things, but rather interrelated threads that weave together to create a beautiful and lasting tapestry of love. As your relationship with God strengthens, so will your relationship with your spouse. As you cultivate your marriage, you will create a fertile ground for spiritual development and shared religious experiences.

This workbook is built upon the foundation of prayer, which is the lifeblood of every Christian marriage. It is the mechanism by which we communicate with God, express our gratitude, seek His guidance, and let go of our burdens. When couples pray together, they bring God into the center of their relationship, creating a sacred space where vulnerability and intimacy can grow. Shared prayer unites hearts, promotes harmony, and strengthens the bond between husband and wife.

However, prayer is more than just a group activity; it is also a personal practice that feeds individual souls and strengthens the link between each couple and God. Praying for your partner is an act of love, a way to express your support, and a powerful tool for intercession. When you bring your spouse's needs, dreams, and struggles to God, you become an active partner in their spiritual journey, walking beside them in faith and offering continual encouragement.

God's Word, the Bible, serves as a compass and guidance for Christian couples seeking to build a marriage that reflects His creation. Studying Scripture together helps you understand God's plan for marriage, His expectations of husbands and wives, and His promises to those who seek Him. The Bible includes timeless wisdom, practical advice, and inspiring anecdotes about couples who tackled marriage obstacles with faith and resilience.

Applying biblical principles to your marriage is essential for creating a strong and lasting foundation. The Bible emphasizes several aspects of married life, including love, forgiveness, communication, and conflict resolution. By studying these principles together and discussing how they apply to your relationship, you will gain valuable insights and skills for navigating marriage's challenges while also appreciating its joys.

Communication, at the heart of connection, is another critical component of a good marriage. It acts as a conduit for couples to communicate their thoughts, feelings, dreams, and concerns. An open and honest conversation fosters understanding, trust, and closeness. When couples communicate well, they create a safe space for vulnerability, making both partners feel heard, valued, and respected.

Active listening is an essential skill for effective communication. It includes not only hearing what your spouse says but also truly understanding the message they are conveying. Active listening involves paying attention to nonverbal cues, asking clarifying questions, and reflecting on what you've heard. When you practice active listening, you demonstrate respect for your partner's point of view and create an environment that encourages open and honest communication.

Honest communication is also essential in a successful marriage. It requires being honest about your thoughts and feelings, even if they are challenging or uncomfortable. Honest expression requires guts, vulnerability, and a willingness to be honest with your relationship. When you express yourself honestly, you make room for deeper connections and understanding.

Marriage, like any other union, is certain to have difficulties. The way couples manage disagreements can either enhance or harm their relationships. Conflict resolution skills are required to peacefully manage arguments and establish solutions that take into account both participants' interests and perspectives.

Fighting honestly includes establishing ground rules for disagreements, avoiding destructive tendencies like personal attacks or blame-shifting, and focusing on finding mutually acceptable solutions. It requires a willingness to compromise, a dedication to understanding your partner's point of view, and a drive to handle disagreements in a way that enhances rather than damages the relationship.

Forgiveness and reconciliation are essential components of conflict resolution in Christian marriage. Holding grudges or resentments can poison a relationship, inhibiting intimacy and hindering spiritual growth. Forgiveness, on the other hand, is a thoughtful and gracious gesture that allows partners to move on from previous hurts and rebuild trust.

Love languages, or the unique ways in which people express and receive love, are key factors in marital satisfaction and intimacy. Understanding your partner's love language allows you to communicate love in a way that is truly meaningful to them, strengthening your emotional bond and creating a sense of being truly known and treasured.

The five basic love languages are affirmation, acts of service, receiving gifts, quality time, and physical touch. Each person has a primary love language that speaks most strongly to their heart. When you learn to communicate in your partner's love language, you replenish their emotional love tank and start a positive feedback cycle of love and appreciation.

Intimacy in marriage goes beyond the physical. It combines emotional, spiritual, and intellectual connections, resulting in a strong and diverse bond between husband and wife. Nurturing intimacy on all levels is essential for a thriving and fulfilling marriage.

Emotional intimacy requires openness, trust, and the willingness to share your most private thoughts and feelings with your spouse. It is about creating a secure space where you can be yourself without fear of being judged or rejected. Emotional closeness enhances your bond and builds a solid foundation of mutual support and understanding.

Spiritual intimacy means discussing your faith journey with your spouse, praying together, studying Scripture, and praising God as a couple. It is about uniting your hearts and seeking God's will for your marriage. When you cultivate spiritual connection, you create a shared spiritual basis that strengthens your relationship and provides stability during difficult times.

Shared goals and objectives are the foundation for a common future. When couples create a vision for their lives together, they receive a sense of purpose and direction, working toward common goals while supporting each other's aspirations.

Vision casting is the process of discussing your future aims, dreams, and goals, both individually and together. It's about creating a road map for your life together, deciding on priorities, and making plans to achieve your shared goals. When you share a vision, you create hope and anticipation for the future, strengthening your bond and fueling your commitment to one another.

Supporting one another's ambitions is essential for personal growth and marital happiness. It requires encouraging your spouse to achieve their goals, providing practical aid, and recognizing their accomplishments. When you support each other's aspirations, you create an environment of mutual respect and empowerment, allowing both partners to prosper and reach their greatest potential.

Finances can cause stress and conflict in a marriage, but they can also give opportunities for collaboration and shared decision-making. Developing a unified approach to finances needs open communication, openness, and a willingness to collaborate on common financial goals.

Budgeting and financial planning are essential for effectively managing your money and avoiding unnecessary stress. Creating a budget allows you to keep track of your income and expenses, identify areas for savings, and make better spending decisions. When you create a budget together, you gain a shared awareness of your financial situation and collaborate to achieve financial stability.

Generosity and giving are fundamental values of Christian marriages. Giving back to your community and supporting causes that you believe in can strengthen your relationship and develop a sense of shared purpose. It's also an opportunity to put your faith into practice and exemplify biblical principles like charity and compassion.

Family and friends are important in our lives, but it is necessary to establish proper boundaries in marriage in order to protect and prioritize your relationship. Building healthy boundaries requires limiting others' influence, outlining your needs clearly, and creating a healthy balance between your marriage and other relationships.

Nurturing supportive relationships outside of marriage may also serve to strengthen your bond as a couple. Surrounding yourself with friends and family who support your relationship and share your values can help you feel encouraged, guided, and a feeling of belonging.

Serving as a couple is a great way to strengthen your relationship, deepen your faith, and make a positive impact in your community. Finding shared ministry opportunities allows you to use your skills and talents to benefit others, establishing a sense of shared purpose and joy.

Making a difference in your community can take many forms, such as volunteering at a local soup kitchen, mentoring young people, and participating in environmental projects. When you serve together, you not only benefit others but also strengthen your ties and connect with your community.

This workbook is more than just a list of tasks and questions; it's a call to a more intimate, joyful marriage. It's a guide for couples looking to connect on a deeper level, communicate more effectively, and leave a lasting legacy of love. It is a roadmap for couples who want to strengthen their bond and create a marriage that honors and reflects God's love.

These sections feature useful advice, engaging tasks, and thought-provoking questions designed to spark meaningful conversations and inspire thoughtful action. You will learn how to pray together, study Scripture, resolve conflicts constructively, and express love in ways that are meaningful to your partner. You'll explore the depths of intimacy, create a shared vision for your future, and discover the power of service together.

This is not a journey to be made alone. It's a shared journey, a dance of two souls seeking to grow in love and faith. As you work through this workbook, remember that you are not only strengthening your marriage; you are also deepening your relationship with God and leaving a loving legacy for future generations.

How to Use This Workbook

This workbook is designed to be an interactive experience, allowing you and your spouse to actively participate in strengthening your marriage and broadening your faith. **Here's how to make the best of it:**

→ Set aside devoted time: Consistency is key. Set up regular time to review the chapters together, whether it's a weekly date night or a few minutes each day.

→ Create a Safe Space: Choose a comfortable, distraction-free environment in which to relax and be open to sharing.

→ Be Honest and Vulnerable: This workbook pushes you to explore complex and timely topics. Approach each task with an open mind and a willingness to be honest with yourself and others.

→ Communicate openly: Feel free to voice your thoughts and feelings. Actively listen to your partner's point of view, even if it differs from your own.

→ Take your time: Don't rush through the workouts. Allow yourself time to reflect, discuss, and completely absorb the ideas.

→ Personalize it: Feel free to tailor the routines to your personal needs and preferences. Add your questions, reflections, and prayers.

→ Celebrate your progress. Recognize and appreciate the efforts you're both making to strengthen your marriage and grow in your faith.

→ Remember Grace: be patient with yourself and others. Growth takes time and will present both obstacles and opportunities. Give grace freely to yourself and your relationship.

This workbook is a tool, but the real work happens in your hearts and through your daily interactions. Use this workbook to spark deeper conversations, deepen intimacy, and strengthen your bond—both with one another and with God.

Chapter 1: Prayer: The Lifeline of Your Marriage

"Devote yourselves to prayer, being watchful and thankful." - Colossians 4:2

Prayer in the context of a Christian marriage is more than just a religious requirement or a rote repetition of words. It is the very lifeblood that flows through the heart of a marriage, connecting husband and wife not only to God but also to the most intimate parts of themselves. It is a sacred exchange, a gathering place where vulnerabilities are shared, fears are exposed, and hopes are elevated together.

When couples prioritize prayer, they introduce a third presence into their marriage: the presence of God. This creates a unique dynamic, a spiritual triangle in which two people become three, linked by a shared religion and a language of love and devotion. Prayer promotes trust in a higher power, recognizing that a strong marriage is built not only through human effort but also through God's love and direction.

Praying as a pair is a symbol of unity. It's a visible expression of your commitment to one another and your shared principles. During tranquil moments of collective prayer, walls fall, defenses crumble, and hearts join. You become a single spiritual entity seeking God's blessings, wisdom, and strength.

This combined prayer does not require elaborate procedures or formal settings. It might be as simple as holding hands before going to bed and saying a thank-you prayer for the day, or as formal as scheduling a full prayer session once per week. The key is to come before God, recognize His sovereignty, and seek His presence in your relationship.

Consistency is key. Marriage, like a plant, needs constant prayer in order to bloom. Making prayer a regular practice, even if only for a few seconds in the middle of life's craziness, can have a tremendous impact on your relationship. It becomes a rhythm, a natural part of your shared existence, much like breathing in fresh air from God's love.

Do not be afraid to experiment with various types of prayer. Read Scripture verses aloud and consider how they pertain to your life. Maintain a prayer notebook to record your petitions, praises, and reflections. Experiment with various prayer approaches, ranging from spontaneous discussions with God to more formal prayers of adoration and confession. Find something that feels authentic and allows you to openly express your emotions.

Individual prayers for one another are an important part of marriage prayer. It's an act of selfless love that shows concern and support for your spouse's well-being. When you pray for your partner, you are simply saying, "I see you, I love you, and I'm entrusting you to God's care."

These prayers can be quite personal and specific. Pray for your spouse's career, health, and mental stability. Please pray for their relationship with family and friends. Pray for their goals, dreams, and anxieties. Pray for their spiritual development, character formation, and connection with God.

Praying for your spouse is not an attempt to control or change them to fit your ideal. It's about entrusting them to God's loving hands, believing that He knows them well and will work in their lives according to His perfect plan. It is about aligning your heart with God's for your spouse, wishing the best for them, and helping them on their spiritual journey.

Praying for your husband can provide inspiration and strength for both of you. Knowing that someone is always praying for you can provide comfort and peace, especially during difficult times. It offers people a sense of being loved, supported, and understood, especially under difficult circumstances.

To develop this habit, set aside time each day or week to pray specifically for your partner. Write down your prayers in a notebook or on a notecard. Each time you pray, concentrate on one area of their lives. As you pray, listen for God's messages of wisdom and encouragement for your spouse.

Praying for each other requires not only asking God to intercede in your spouse's life but also deepening your understanding of them. As you pray, you will learn about their aspirations, fears, and desires. You'll develop greater empathy and compassion as you learn to see the world through their eyes and appreciate their unique perspective.

This better understanding might result in more intimacy and connection in your marriage. You'll be more aware of your spouse's needs, more sensitive to their struggles, and better able to offer support and encouragement. You'll also be more likely to communicate effectively, resolve problems constructively, and build better, longer-lasting connections.

Prayer does not resolve all marital issues. However, it is a powerful motivator for transformation, growth, and healing. It is a technique of inviting God's presence into your home, heart, and daily interactions. It's a way to align your goals with His, seek His guidance, and trust in His plan for your marriage.

When you make prayer a priority, you will learn that it is about changing your heart as much as your circumstances. It is about increasing dependence on God, being more aware of His presence, and making a firmer commitment to living out your faith in the context of your marriage.

Prayer is a personal language that shows vulnerability while also offering strength and guidance. It is the lifeblood that binds a Christian marriage together, uniting husband and wife and the heart of God. By incorporating prayer into the fabric of your relationship, you will create a tapestry of love, faith, and resilience that will withstand the test of time and shine brightly for His glory.

The quiet moments of group prayer offer a refuge from the world's noise and distractions. You'll form stronger bonds with one another and with the One who created and brought you together. You'll experience the peace that passes understanding, the joy that comes from walking beside God, and the love that binds two hearts together for eternity.

Praying Together

Praying as a couple is a deeply intimate act. It acknowledges that you are more than just two people going through life together; you are a partnership, a unified force seeking God's presence and direction. When you pray together, you create a sacred space in which vulnerabilities are acknowledged, concerns are shared, and hopes are elevated in harmony.

Shared prayer is an invitation to intimacy. It is a shedding of pretense, a lowering of defenses, and a gathering of hearts before the Divine. During tranquil moments of combined prayer, walls dissolve, masks fall away, and you connect on a deeper level. You see each other as more than just spouses but as spiritual comrades on a quest to uncover God's Light.

This relationship is more than just emotional; it is spiritual. When you pray together, you bring God into the center of your relationship. You acknowledge His sovereignty, seek His guidance, and align your wills with His larger plan. This shared surrender creates a relationship that transcends the physical and emotional, bringing you together in a spiritual dance of love and dedication.

Praying together doesn't require sophisticated procedures or formal settings. It may be as simple as holding hands before a meal and praying for thanks, or as structured as setting aside time each day for a full prayer session. The key is consistency, making prayer a natural and significant part of your shared life.

Consider it like breathing. Prayer, like breathing, can become a natural rhythm in your marriage, providing a consistent flow of communication with God. This ongoing connection strengthens your bond and provides a spiritual foundation during life's storms.

To establish this routine, consider setting aside time for a couple of prayers. Perhaps it's a few minutes in the morning before the day's responsibilities take over, or a relaxing night routine before retiring. Perhaps it's a weekly "prayer date" in which you purposefully avoid distractions and concentrate on connecting with God and one another.

Don't be afraid to try new ways to pray. Read Scripture aloud and consider how it applies to your life and relationships. Maintain a prayer notebook to record your petitions, praises, and reflections. Experiment with various prayer approaches, ranging from spontaneous discussions with God to more formal prayers of adoration and confession. Find something that resonates with both of you and allows you to truly express your souls.

Here are some examples of several prayer styles and formats that you can use in your shared prayer session:

- Conversational Prayer: Talk to God like you would a trusted friend, sharing your joys, concerns, and requests in a natural, conversational tone.

- Scripture-Based Prayer: Pray through specific Bible passages, allowing the words of Scripture to guide and inspire your heart.

- Adoration and Praise: In your prayers, show your love and admiration for God, acknowledge His attributes, and thank Him for His blessings.

- Confession and Repentance: Take time to confess your faults to God, both individually and as a couple, and beg for forgiveness and cleansing.

- Intercession: Pray for others, including family, friends, your community, and the whole world.

- Silent Prayer: Spend some time in quiet thought, listening for God's voice and allowing Him to speak into your hearts.

The beauty of prayer is that there is no right or wrong way to do it. The most important thing is to approach God with a pure heart, open to His presence and direction. Making prayer a regular part of your marriage will bring you closer to each other and God's heart.

Praying for Each Other

In the tranquil intimacy of your prayer time, when it's just you and God, you have a unique opportunity to petition for the person you care most about: your spouse. Individual prayer for your spouse is an expression of sincere love and support, expressing care, concern, and a great desire for their well-being. It is a spiritual act of service, a selfless offering from your heart to God in their name.

When you pray for your spouse, you are essentially saying, "I see you, I love you, and I'm lifting you to the One who loves you most." You recognize their humanity, problems, dreams, and distinct spiritual paths. You are working with God in their lives, seeking His guidance, protection, and supply.

Individual prayer for your spouse is a powerful display of love. It indicates your genuine concern for their well-being, not only physically and emotionally, but also spiritually. You're expressing a wish for them to strengthen their relationship with God, to experience His peace and joy, and to follow His will for their lives.

Praying for your spouse is also an expression of support. It's a method to help them through their difficulties, encourage them to reach their goals, and celebrate their accomplishments. When you pray for them, you provide them with a spiritual safety net, a constant reminder that they are not alone on this road.

This intimate prayer time can provide you both with strength and peace. Knowing that someone is continually praying for you can bring a sense of peace and security, especially during difficult times. It can also encourage you to persevere in your spiritual journey, knowing that you have a spouse praying for your advancement and well-being.

Make praying for your spouse a regular practice by setting aside time each day or week for this purpose. It could be a few minutes in the morning before you start your day, a tranquil moment during your lunch break, or a specific time in the evening before bed.

As you pray, focus on specific parts of your spouse's life. Pray for their bodily well-being, mental stability, and spiritual growth. Please pray for their careers, relationships, and ambitions. Please pray for their concerns, anxieties, hopes, and dreams.

Here are a few ideas and questions to assist you pray for your spouse:

Spiritual Growth:

- Pray for your spouse to grow in their relationship with God.
- Please pray to God to reveal Himself to your spouse in new and meaningful ways.
- Pray for your spouse to develop a better understanding of God's Word and His plan for their life.
- Pray for your spouse to be filled with the Holy Spirit and to demonstrate the Fruit of the Spirit.

Emotional wellbeing:

- Pray that your partner will discover peace, joy, and contentment.
- When your companion is agitated or anxious, ask God to comfort them.
- Pray for your spouse's wisdom and discernment in making decisions.
- Pray that your partner is free of fear, worry, and negativity.

Physical Health:

- Pray for your spouse's physical health and strength.
- Ask God to protect your spouse from illness and injury.
- Pray for your spouse's energy and vitality.

- Pray for your spouse to make healthy choices and care for their body.

Work and Career:

- Pray for your spouse's work and profession.
- Please ask God to bless your spouse with success and fulfillment at work.
- Pray for your spouse's wisdom and judgment as they make work-related decisions.
- Pray that your spouse will have a beneficial impact in their workplace.

Relationships:

- Pray for your spouse's relationships with family and friends.
- Ask God to bless your marriage with healthy and supportive relationships.
- Pray for your husband's love and forgiveness.
- Pray that your husband will be an effective listener and communicator.

Dreams and Aspirations:

- Pray for your spouse's hopes and goals.
- Ask God to give your spouse the courage and motivation to pursue their goals.
- Pray for your spouse to be successful in achieving their goals.
- Pray that your spouse finds fulfillment and significance in their lives.

Challenges and Struggles:

- Pray for your spouse's difficulties and struggles.
- Ask God to give your spouse the strength and endurance to overcome adversity.
- Pray that your spouse finds comfort and peace amid adversity.
- Pray that your spouse will learn and grow from their problems.

Remember that by praying for your spouse, you are cooperating with God in their lives. You are not striving to control or change them, but rather to entrust them to God's loving care and faith in His plan for their lives.

Praying for your spouse is a show of love, support, and faith. It's an opportunity to strengthen, develop, and grow your relationship with God. As you include this practice into your daily life, you will learn how prayer may benefit not only your spouse's life but also your own.

<u>**Key Points**</u>

- Prayer is essential for a healthy and successful Christian marriage. It promotes a deeper relationship with God and one another.

- Praying as a couple fosters togetherness, closeness, and a common spiritual experience.

- Praying for your spouse individually expresses love, support, and concern for their well-being.

- Consistency in prayer, both together and individually, is critical to developing a strong spiritual tie in your marriage.

- There are many different styles and formats of prayer. Discover what works best for your relationship and be open to new ideas.

<u>**Self-Reflection Questions**</u>

1. How often do you pray with your partner? How can you incorporate prayer into your daily routine more regularly?

____

____

____

____

____

2. Do you and your partner feel joined and connected when you pray? Why/why not?

____

____

____

____

____

3. How do you typically pray for your spouse individually? What specific parts of their lives may you address in your prayers?

____

____

____

____

4. In what ways has prayer impacted your marriage and relationship with God?

____

____

____

____

5. What challenges do you have in making prayer a priority in your marriage? How will you handle these challenges?

____

____

____

____

Chapter 2: God's Word

"All Scripture is God-breathed and is useful for teaching, rebuking, correcting and training in righteousness, so that the servant of God may be thoroughly equipped for every good work." - 2 Timothy 3:16-17

In the journey of a Christian marriage, God's Word serves as a compass and guide, illuminating the path to a love established on faith, purpose, and lasting strength. It is a source of information, comfort, and education, offering timeless ideals and practical counsel for dealing with the challenges of married life while also enjoying the pleasures.

When couples open their hearts and minds to biblical reality, they powerfully invite God's presence into their relationship. They acknowledge His authority, seek His guidance, and let His Word shape their thoughts, attitudes, and actions. This shared commitment to God's Word provides a spiritual foundation for the marriage, allowing them to create a life together that honors and reflects His love.

Couples who read Scripture together display unity and a common purpose. It recognizes that you are more than just two people reading the same book; you are a spiritual team seeking to understand God's plan for your lives and marriage. When you read the Bible together, you create a sacred space where everyone may learn, grow, and be challenged.

This shared study is an invitation to intimacy. It's a peeling back of layers that reveals hearts and minds as you discuss God's Word and how it applies to your relationships. In the vulnerability of combined study, you see each other not just as spouses, but as companions on a spiritual journey seeking truth and understanding together.

The act of studying the Bible together does not require specialist theology degrees or rigorous schedules. It could be as simple as reading a passage aloud every day and discussing how it speaks to you, or as structured as following a specific Bible study plan or devotional guide. The key is consistency, therefore make Bible study a regular and necessary part of your family routine.

Consider cultivating a garden. A marriage, like a garden, needs consistent nourishment from God's Word in order to grow strong and alive. This daily feeding of your spirits will strengthen your bond, providing spiritual sustenance and guidance in the face of life's challenges and joys.

To cultivate this habit, try committing time each week to Bible study as a couple. Perhaps it's a nice evening after dinner, a weekend morning with coffee and conversation, or a relaxing lunch break somewhere. Find a regimen that works for you and stick to it, making it an essential part of your week.

Do not be afraid to experiment with different Bible study methods. Read a book of the Bible together, verse by verse, and discuss your discoveries and questions. Look into topical studies that address specific issues in your marriage, such as communication, conflict resolution, and intimacy. Begin a discussion and present various perspectives on Scripture using devotional literature or internet resources.

The beauty of studying the Bible together is that it is an exploration of God's truth and how it applies to your lives. It's an opportunity to learn from one another, challenge one another, and deepen your understanding of God's Word and His plan for your marriage.

Applying biblical principles to your marriage is essential for creating a strong and lasting foundation. The Bible is more than just a collection of stories and lessons; it is a living document that tackles the most fundamental aspects of human life, including the ups and downs of marriage.

When you actively seek to incorporate biblical principles into your relationship, you are effectively allowing God to create your marriage. You've accepted that His methods are greater than yours, His ideas are higher than yours, and His marital plan is the blueprint for a fulfilling and God-honoring relationship.

The Bible addresses a variety of marriage-related issues, including love, forgiveness, communication, conflict resolution, and intimacy. By studying these principles together and discussing how they apply to your relationship, you can gain valuable insights and techniques for navigating the complexities of marriage while also enjoying its pleasures.

For example, the Bible describes love as patient, sympathetic, and selfless. It is not easily angered, has no history of wrongdoing, and always protects, trusts, hopes, and perseveres. When you apply this concept of love to your marriage, you build a foundation of grace, forgiveness, and unwavering dedication.

The Bible emphasizes the need for forgiveness in marriage. It teaches us how to forgive one another, just as Christ forgives us. Forgiveness is not a feeling; it is a decision, an act of obedience to God's instructions, and a demonstration of His love for humanity. When you choose to forgive your spouse, you release the bitterness and resentment that may poison a relationship, making way for healing and reconciliation.

Communication is another area where biblical ideas can help guide and improve your marriage. The Bible instructs us to be quick to listen, slow to speak, and slow to become angry. It encourages us to speak the truth in love, to promote one another by our words, and to avoid gossip, slander, and harsh criticism. When you apply these principles to your communication, you promote a culture of respect, understanding, and genuine connection.

Conflict is natural in any relationship, but the Bible teaches how to handle it in a way that honors God and strengthens your bond. It instructs us not to let the sun go down while we are still angry, to be kind and empathetic to one another, and to seek peace and reconciliation wherever possible. When you apply these concepts to conflict resolution, you create a pattern of effective communication and mutual respect.

Intimacy is another area where biblical principles can help improve and strengthen your marriage. The Bible recognizes the beauty and purity of sexual intimacy in marriage while emphasizing the importance of emotional and spiritual connection. When you approach intimacy through the lens of Scripture, you can have a healthy and enjoyable sex life that honors God while simultaneously enhancing your relationship.

Applying biblical principles to your marriage is allowing God's Word to shape your hearts, attitudes, and actions rather than merely following a set of rules and regulations. It is about seeking His wisdom and guidance in all parts of your relationship, from the routine to the monumental.

As you study the Bible together and discuss how its teachings apply to your marriage, you'll discover that God's Word is a living, active force that can alter your relationship from the inside out. It offers strength, comfort, and guidance, leading you to a relationship based on faith, purpose, and enduring strength.

Studying Scripture as a Couple

Reading and studying the Bible as a couple is more than just religious observance; it is a purposeful choice to bring God's presence into the center of your relationship. It acknowledges that your marriage is built not only on human connection and shared dreams but also on the timeless wisdom and enduring truths of God's word.

When you open the Bible together, you are not just reading words on a page; you are engaging in a spiritual discourse. You are allowing God to speak into your hearts, challenge your beliefs, and bring you to a love that mirrors His own. This shared experience creates a special bond, a spiritual connection that strengthens your relationship and develops your personal faith journeys.

Studying the Bible together fosters a sense of community and shared purpose. You are more than just husband and wife; you are fellow students, learning and growing together as you understand God's love, His plan for your lives, and His design for marriage. You're on a voyage of discovery together, seeking truth and knowledge while also supporting one another's spiritual growth.

This collaborative quest for knowledge also promotes intimacy. It's an invitation to be vulnerable, a safe space to share your thoughts, concerns, and insights as you work through the book and its implications for your life. You can be honest about your struggles, uncertainties, and hopes while studying the Bible with others, knowing that you are completely accepted and loved.

This vulnerability strengthens your link, allowing you to see each other not only as spouses but as fellow travelers on a spiritual journey. You become witnesses to each other's growth, providing encouragement and support as you both strive to live your faith in a way that honors God and strengthens your marriage.

Studying the Bible together can also provide comfort and strength, particularly during tough times. When life throws you curveballs, the Bible may provide consolation, counsel, and hope through its stories of redemption and endurance.

Consider setting aside time each week for Bible study. Perhaps it's a nice evening after dinner, a weekend morning with coffee and conversation, or a relaxing lunch break somewhere. Find a rhythm that works for you and adhere to it, making it an essential part of your weekly routine.

Do not be afraid to experiment with different Bible study methods. Here are some tips to get you started:

- Topical Studies: Choose a topic relevant to your marriage, such as communication, conflict resolution, finances, or intimacy. Then, look for Bible passages that address the subject and discuss them together. This focused approach may help you apply biblical teachings to specific elements of your relationship.

- Book studies involve reading through a book of the Bible together, chapter by chapter, verse by verse. This allows you to have a greater understanding of a book's context and message, as well as how its themes apply to your personal life and marriage.

- Devotional Reading Plans: Using a devotional guide or an internet resource, provide daily readings and reflections on specific biblical passages. This can be a good method for staying consistent in your Bible study while also learning new things from different authors and views.

- Character studies entail studying the life and experiences of a biblical figure like Abraham, Moses, Ruth, or Esther. Discuss how their story relates to your own, and what lessons you might glean from their faith and obedience.

- Word Studies: Select a word or phrase from the Bible that calls to you, such as "love," "grace," "forgiveness," or "peace." Look up the definition in a Bible dictionary or concordance, then look into how the word is used throughout Scripture. This can help you better appreciate the scope and intricacies of God's Word.

Whatever technique you choose, bear in mind that the goal is not simply to study, but also to let God's Word shape your hearts and minds. While studying together, ask yourself:

- How does this chapter speak to us individually?
- How does this apply to our marriage?
- What is God teaching us through this passage?
- How can we apply these facts to our daily lives?

Creating a shared space for learning and reflection is essential for a successful Bible study session. Find a comfortable and tranquil location in which you can concentrate without distractions. Gather your Bibles, notebooks, pens, and any other supplies you might need. To set a peaceful atmosphere, consider lighting a candle or playing soothing music.

Most importantly, begin your study sessions with an open heart and mind. Be willing to listen, ask questions, and challenge one another's perspectives. Remember that you are both on a journey of learning and growth and that God's Word is a powerful tool for transformation and connection.

Applying Biblical Principles to Your Marriage

The Bible is more than just a collection of historical accounts and moral precepts; it's a living, breathing guide to life, offering everlasting wisdom and practical instruction for every aspect of human experience, including the complicated dance of marriage. When couples intentionally seek to apply biblical principles to their relationship, they are essentially enabling God to create their love, the foundation upon which they will build a life together.

This application of biblical principles is not about following a rigid set of rules or regulations, but about allowing God's Word to penetrate your hearts, thoughts, and actions. It is about realizing that His ways are superior to ours, His thoughts are higher than ours, and His design for marriage is the blueprint for a fulfilling and God-honoring partnership.

The Bible speaks volumes about love, offering a definition that goes well beyond fleeting emotions and beautiful gestures. In 1 Corinthians 13, love is described as patient, sympathetic, and selfless. It is not easily angered, has no history of wrongdoing, and always protects, trusts, hopes, and perseveres. This is the kind of love God wants us to cultivate in our marriages: unshakeable, unconditional, and firmly anchored in His grace.

To implement this definition of love in your marriage, you must be intentional and make an effort. It requires deciding to be patient with your partner, even if they are difficult to grasp. It entails being kind even when you feel wronged. It means putting others' needs before your own, even if it is uncomfortable. It entails forgiving freely, as Christ did for you.

Forgiveness is another crucial component of a strong Christian marriage, and it appears throughout Scripture. Ephesians 4:32 says, "Be kind and compassionate to one another, forgiving one another, just as God forgave you." Forgiveness is not an emotion; it is a choice, an act of obedience to God's instructions, and a show of His deep love for us.

Choosing to forgive your spouse, even if it is difficult, is an act of letting go of the resentment and anger that may poison a relationship. It's a way to disrupt the cycle of hurt while simultaneously promoting healing and reconciliation. It recognizes that we all make mistakes, fall short, and need God's grace and forgiveness to move forward.

Communication is crucial in any relationship, and the Bible offers valuable guidance on how to communicate effectively in marriage. James 1:19 says we should be "quick to listen, slow to speak, and slow to become angry." This simple but important lesson encourages us to have talks with humility, tolerance, and a genuine desire to understand our spouse's point of view.

Applying this concept to your communication includes actively listening to your spouse, even if you disagree. It requires taking the time to examine their point of view, even if it is different from yours. It requires choosing your words carefully, telling the truth with compassion, and avoiding harsh criticism or judgment.

Conflict is natural in any relationship, but the Bible offers advice on how to settle them in a way that honors God and strengthens your bond. In Ephesians 4:26, we are warned, "In your anger, do not sin; do not let the sun go down while you are angry." This paragraph emphasizes the importance of resolving conflicts quickly and in a healthy manner.

To use this method in your marriage, you must be prepared to tackle issues rather than ignore them. It requires communicating your expectations and concerns directly and respectfully, as well as being willing to understand your spouse's point of view. It requires working toward reconciliation and repair, even when it is difficult.

Intimacy is another area where biblical principles can help improve and strengthen your marriage. The Bible recognizes the beauty and purity of sexual intimacy in marriage while emphasizing the importance of emotional and spiritual connection. The Song of Solomon shows a beautiful portrayal of love and intimacy between a husband and wife, one that is passionate, playful, and emotionally rewarding.

Applying this biblical concept of intimacy to your marriage includes viewing sex as a sacred act, a gift from God that should be experienced and treasured within the context of marriage. It means appreciating emotional and spiritual ties and recognizing that true intimacy goes well beyond the physical realm. It comprises open and honest discussions about your wants and desires, creating a safe environment for vulnerability and shared delight.

To help you apply these biblical principles to your marriage, consider the following exercises:

1. Love in Action:

- Choose one paragraph from 1 Corinthians 13 that speaks to you about love.
- Discuss how you may incorporate this concept of love into your daily interactions with one another.
- Make a list of specific actions you may take to show your spouse love in a way that is compatible with this biblical definition.

2) Forgiveness Challenge:

- Consider a time when you were injured or wronged by your relationship.
- Discuss how to forgive someone even when you don't want to.
- Write a prayer of forgiveness for your spouse, asking God to help you let go of any resentment or anger.

3. Communication Check-Up

- Evaluate your couple's communication habits.
- Discuss how you can improve your listening skills and communicate more effectively.
- Commit to actively listening and speaking the truth in love.

4. Conflict Resolution Roadmap:

- Describe a recent dispute in your relationship.
- Discuss how you may have handled the issue differently, utilizing Christian themes like forgiveness, communication, and reconciliation.
- Create a "conflict resolution plan" that outlines positive strategies for future arguments.

5. Intimacy Inventory:

- Discuss your understanding of intimacy in light of biblical teachings.
- Investigate techniques to improve your emotional, spiritual, and physical relationships.

- Make a strategy to prioritize intimacy in your marriage, setting up specific times for connection and communication.

Remember that integrating biblical principles in your marriage is an ongoing effort, not a one-time event. It requires commitment, effort, and a desire to learn and grow together. As you continue to seek God's knowledge and guidance through His Word, you will see that your marriage reflects His love, demonstrates His grace, and provides strength and joy for both of you.

Key Points

- The Bible is an excellent resource for couples seeking to build a strong, God-centered marriage. It offers counsel, expertise, and support as you face the challenges and joys of marriage.

- Studying the Bible together promotes a shared spiritual experience, strengthens your bond, and helps you grasp God's plan for your marriage.

- Applying biblical principles to your relationship allows you to build a strong foundation on God's design for marriage.

- Consistency in Bible study, both individually and as a couple, is critical for spiritual growth and a deeper connection with God.

- There are various methods for studying the Bible. Discover what works best for you as a couple and be prepared to try new ideas.

Self-Reflection Questions

1. How often do you read or study the Bible with your spouse? What are some tips for making Bible study a more regular part of your routine?

____

____

____

____

____

2. What is your preferred method of Bible study, both individually and as a couple? What new approaches do you want to try?

____

____

____

____

____

3. How do you generally apply biblical principles in your marriage? Which specific features could you improve?

____

____

____

____

____

4. What are some of the challenges you face when making Bible study a priority in your marriage? How will you handle these challenges?

____

____

____

____

____

5. How has studying the Bible together benefited your marriage and personal connections with God?

____

____

____

____

____

Chapter 3: Communication: The Heart of Connection

"My dear brothers and sisters, take note of this: Everyone should be quick to listen, slow to speak and slow to become angry." - James 1:19

Communication, in its purest form, is the lifeblood of any successful relationship, and nowhere is this more evident than in the sacred bond of marriage. It is the link between two hearts, the language that enables the interchange of thoughts, feelings, dreams, and fears. A strong and successful marriage is built on open, honest, and respectful communication that facilitates understanding, intimacy, and mutual improvement.

When couples prioritize communication, they create a safe space for vulnerability, making both partners feel heard, valued, and respected. They establish trust, allowing thoughts and feelings to be expressed without fear of being judged or rejected. They promote an empathetic culture in which both partners attempt to understand the other's point of view, even if they disagree.

Effective communication entails more than just talking; it also requires active listening. It entails paying attention not just to the words spoken, but also to the nonverbal cues, body language, and emotions that follow them. It is about understanding your spouse's heart, grasping their perspective, and empathizing with their experiences.

Active listening is an excellent way to promote connection and understanding in marriage. It requires being fully present in the moment, paying close attention to your spouse, and making a genuine effort to hear and comprehend their message. It's about putting aside your views and distractions and focusing on truly absorbing what your spouse is saying.

Active listening entails more than just hearing words; it also requires observing nonverbal cues including facial expressions, body language, and tone of voice. It is about asking clarifying questions to ensure you get your message correctly. It's about reflecting on what you've heard to strengthen your comprehension and demonstrate that you're fully engaged in the conversation.

When you practice active listening, you create a safe environment in which your partner may express themselves fully and honestly. You respect their thoughts and feelings, even if you disagree with them. You establish trust and closeness, laying the groundwork for a deeper connection.

Honest expression is another critical component of healthy marital communication. It means being willing to share your thoughts and feelings openly, even if it is difficult or uncomfortable. It means being vulnerable with your spouse and believing that they will respond with love and understanding.

Honest expression requires guts, and a willingness to step beyond your comfort zone and share the most intimate sides of yourself with your spouse. It entails trust, the belief that your spouse will accept you for who you are, imperfections included. It requires a commitment to open and honest communication, especially when it is challenging.

When you express yourself honestly, you allow for deeper connection and intimacy in your marriage. You allow your spouse to truly know you, understand your feelings, and share in your joys and sorrows. You create a safe space for mutual growth and support, allowing you to be yourself without fear of being judged or rejected.

Effective communication is not always easy, particularly when there are disagreements or strong emotions. However, in these challenging circumstances, communication is much more crucial. Open and honest communication enables you to constructively resolve conflict, find common ground, and emerge from disagreements with a stronger and more resilient friendship.

Here are some practical techniques to increase communication inside your marriage:

- Set a regular time for connecting. Make time for critical connections, such as daily check-ins, weekly date evenings, or weekend getaways.

- Create a safe space for conversation. Choose a comfortable, distraction-free environment in which to relax and share freely.

- Practice active listening. Pay attention to your spouse's words, nonverbal cues, and emotions. Ask clarifying questions and think about what you've heard.

- Express yourself honestly and respectfully. Share your thoughts and feelings openly, but avoid accusing, condemning, or attacking your partner.

- Use "I" statements to express your emotions. This permits you to control your emotions without making your spouse feel defensive.

- Focus on understanding rather than just being understood. Even if you disagree, attempt to comprehend your partner's point of view.

- Take breaks when needed. If a conversation becomes heated or pointless, take a break and resume it later, when you're both more comfortable.

- Pray for guidance. Ask God to help you communicate effectively and strengthen your relationship via open and honest discussions.

Remember that communication is an ongoing process, not a destination. It requires effort, intention, and a desire to learn and grow together. When you prioritize communication in your marriage, you will develop a deeper connection, a stronger bond, and a more meaningful partnership.

Effective communication is more than just avoiding confrontation; it is also about celebrating successes, sharing dreams, and providing support. It is about showing gratitude, admiration, and love to your partner. It's about telling a shared story of two interwoven lives in which each partner feels heard, valued, and cherished.

As you foster an open and honest communication culture in your marriage, you will find that it becomes a source of strength, resilience, and joy. You'll build a safe sanctuary where you can both be yourselves, grow together, and let your love bloom. You'll lay the groundwork for trust and intimacy that will see you through life's struggles and joys.

Active Listening

Active listening is an elegant companion in the complex dance of communication, clearing the way for comprehension, connection, and increased closeness. It's more than just hearing the words spoken; it's a complete commitment to your partner, a willingness to enter their world and see things from their perspective.

Active listening is the foundation for healthy marital communication. It is the link between two hearts, allowing for a genuine exchange of ideas, emotions, and experiences. When you actively listen to your partner, you are expressing, "I value you, I care about what you have to say, and I'm fully present with you in this moment."

This attentive presence is a gift, a worthwhile investment of your time and energy in your relationship. It expresses respect and demonstrates that you value their opinions and feelings. When you actively listen, you create a safe environment in which your spouse may express themselves freely and openly, without fear of being criticized or interrupted.

Active listening employs a multimodal approach, utilizing both verbal and nonverbal clues to create a pleasurable encounter. It is critical to pay attention to not only the words spoken, but also the unspoken language of emotions, body language, and tone of voice.

Nonverbal communication is an important aspect of active listening. Your body language communicates volumes about your level of participation and interest in the conversation. Maintaining eye contact, leaning in slightly, and nodding your head are all nonverbal cues that show your interest and encourage your companion to keep talking.

Paraphrasing is an essential component of active listening. This includes summarizing what you've heard in your own words, confirming your comprehension, and demonstrating that you're actively engaged in the discussion. Paraphrasing helps your spouse to clarify any misunderstandings or provide further information, ensuring that their message is understood accurately.

Active listening is largely built on empathy. It is the ability to put yourself in your spouse's shoes, feel their emotions, and see the world from their perspective. Empathy is not about agreeing with or accepting your spouse's conduct; rather, it is about understanding their emotional condition and offering compassion and support.

When you listen with empathy, you build a stronger bond with your partner. You demonstrate that you care about their feelings, even if you don't fully understand them. You build trust and connection, creating the foundation for a more enjoyable and supportive relationship.

Active listening requires effort, focus, and a genuine desire to understand your spouse. It involves putting aside your thoughts and distractions and focusing your entire attention on the person in front of you. It's about being there, both physically and emotionally.

Here are some useful exercises to help you develop your active listening skills:

- The Mirroring Exercise involves taking turns sharing a thought or emotion. After one person speaks, the other "mirrors" what they heard by summarizing it in their own words. This encourages good comprehension and demonstrates that you are truly listening.

- The Nonverbal Cue Challenge: Pay close attention to your spouse's nonverbal cues when conversing. Examine their facial expressions, body language, and tone of speech. Discuss how these nonverbal cues reinforce their overall message.

- The Empathy Exercise: Share your personal experiences. After one person has shared, the other person tries to show empathy by acknowledging their feelings and offering support. This allows you to try putting yourself in your spouse's position and understanding their emotional state.

- The "Just Listen" Challenge: Set aside time each day or week to simply listen to your partner, without interruption. Instead of offering advice or solutions, focus on listening and comprehending their thoughts and feelings.

Remember that active listening is not about addressing problems or finding solutions; it is about creating a safe environment in which your spouse may be heard and understood. It is about connecting, increasing intimacy, and improving your relationship via attentive presence and genuine empathy.

As you practice active listening, you will discover that it is a powerful tool for communication and connection in your marriage. You'll grow closer, form a stronger bond, and have a more meaningful connection. You'll also have the pleasure of truly knowing and being known by your lover, which is a gift that will strengthen and deepen your relationship for years to come.

Honest Expression

Genuine expression serves as the cornerstone of authentic intimacy in the sacred space of marriage when two lives connect and hearts seek comfort in one another. It is the daring act of sharing your true self, the unfiltered ideas, feelings, and needs that are within. It is the willingness to be vulnerable, to let your guard down, and to trust that your partner will respond to your words with love and understanding.

Honest conversation isn't always easy. It requires courage to step beyond your comfort zone, confront your fears and doubts, and speak your truth, even if it is difficult or uncomfortable. It requires faith in your connection, the belief that they will embrace you for who you are, flaws, and all.

However, the advantages of honest expression are enormous. When you communicate openly and authentically with your partner, you create a stronger bond based on mutual understanding and respect. You allow your spouse to truly understand you, to see into the depths of your heart, and to share your joys and sorrows.

Honest expression entails not only sharing good emotions, but also being willing to express unpleasant emotions such as wrath, grief, and fear. It is about understanding your wants and communicating them to your partner transparently and respectfully. It's about creating a safe space where you can be vulnerable without being judged or rejected.

Expressing painful emotions might be challenging, especially if you were raised in a culture that discouraged openness and suppressed feelings. You may be concerned that expressing your true feelings may end in confrontation, rejection, or injury. However, suppressing your feelings can lead to anger, isolation, and a communication breakdown.

When you can express difficult emotions healthily and productively, you create the possibility of deeper connection and understanding in your marriage. You allow your spouse to see the real you, the person behind the mask, and they show you support and comfort. You also allow your spouse to express their own emotions, which creates a stronger sense of connection and vulnerability in your relationship.

Here are some tools and strategies for communicating assertively and respectfully:

- Use "I" statements to express your emotions. This permits you to manage your emotions without criticizing or condemning your partner. For example, rather than saying, "You always make me angry," say, "I feel angry when..."

- Be specific about your needs and expectations. Do not expect your partner to read your thoughts. Communicate what you require and expect from them in a specific situation.

- Be mindful of your tone of voice and body language. Your nonverbal cues can communicate as effectively as your words. Make sure your tone and body language are consistent with your message.

- Choose an acceptable time and place to communicate. Avoid having uncomfortable conversations while weary, stressed, or preoccupied. Find a calm, private location where you can both concentrate on the subject.

- Be willing to compromise. Remember that healthy communication involves both giving and taking. Be willing to listen to your partner and find solutions that will benefit both of you.

- Practice forgiveness. Everyone makes errors. Be willing to forgive your partner when they hurt you, and ask for forgiveness when you damage them.

- Pray for guidance. Ask God to help you communicate effectively and create a secure space for honest expression in your marriage.

Honest expression does not entail perfection but rather requires sincerity. It's about creating a space in your marriage where you can both be yourselves without fear of being judged or rejected. It is about creating the framework for trust and connection, which will carry you through life's challenges and rewards.

As you prioritize honest expression in your marriage, you will not only strengthen your bond with your spouse but also increase your relationship with God, who created you in His image and desires you to experience the fullness of genuine connection and love.

<u>Key Points</u>

- Communication is the foundation of a successful and happy marriage. It allows you to connect with your partner at a deeper level, build trust, and effectively resolve issues.

- Active listening is essential to effective communication. It involves being completely present, paying attention to verbal and nonverbal cues, and seeking to understand your spouse's point of view.

- Honest expression is essential for building intimacy and trust in your marriage. It means speaking your views and feelings openly, especially when it is difficult.

- Assertive communication enables you to express your needs and opinions clearly and courteously, without appearing aggressive or passive.

- Healthy communication requires effort, intent, and a desire to learn and grow together.

Self-Reflection Questions

1. How do you communicate as a pair now? Are you satisfied with the level of transparency and honesty in your communication?

____

____

____

____

2. How well do you actively listen when your partner speaks? What are some ways to improve your listening skills?

____

____

____

____

3. How comfortable are you expressing your true ideas and feelings to your partner, especially when confronted with difficult emotions or needs?

____

____

____

____

4. How do you generally deal with fights or conflicts in your marriage? Can you talk assertively and respectfully while trying to resolve this?

____

____

____

____

5. What specific steps can you take to improve communication in your marriage and create a safe environment for open and honest conversations?

____

____

____

____

Chapter 4: Conflict Resolution

"Let all bitterness and wrath and anger and clamor and slander be put away from you, along with all malice. Be kind to one another, tenderhearted, forgiving one another, as God in Christ forgave you." -
Ephesians 4:31-32

Conflict, like changing tides, is unavoidable in any relationship, and marriage is no exception. It is the natural ebb and flow of two people with opposing perspectives, personalities, and experiences joining forces to form a life. Confrontation can be uncomfortable, but it is not always negative. In actuality, when handled effectively, debate may promote growth, understanding, and a stronger bond.

Conflict resolution in Christian marriages includes a spiritual component. It is more than just reaching an agreement or settling a conflict; it is about demonstrating Christ's love and forgiveness in your dealings with your spouse, even if you disagree. It is about seeking harmony and understanding, not victory or domination.

The Bible includes a wealth of information on how to resolve disagreements in a healthy and God-honoring manner. It teaches us to be quick to listen, slow to speak, and slow to anger. It encourages us to speak the truth in love, to be kind and compassionate to one another, and to freely forgive, as Christ did for us.

Applying these biblical principles to conflict resolution in your marriage necessitates approaching disagreements with humility, patience, and a genuine desire to understand your spouse's perspective. It means choosing your words carefully and avoiding harsh criticism or judgment. It requires working toward reconciliation and repair, even when it is difficult.

One of the most important aspects of dispute resolution is learning how to "fight fair." This includes establishing ground rules for disagreements, avoiding harmful behaviors like personal attacks or blame-shifting, and focusing on mutually accepted solutions. It requires a willingness to compromise, a dedication to understanding your partner's point of view, and a drive to handle disagreements in a way that enhances rather than damages the relationship.

Here are some key elements of "fighting fair":

- Maintain your composure and respect. Avoid raising your voice, shouting insults, or launching personal attacks.

- Focus on the task at hand. Avoid bringing up old grievances or other issues.

- Use "I" statements to express your emotions. This permits you to control your emotions without making your spouse feel defensive.

- Be willing to hear your spouse's point of view. Try to understand their point of view, even if you disagree with it.

- Take breaks when needed. If a conversation becomes heated or pointless, take a break and resume it later, when you're both more comfortable.

- Seek compromise and solutions. Look for win-win solutions that address both your needs and worries.

- Finish with forgiveness and reconciliation. Get rid of any hate and hatred, and make a concerted effort to go forward.

Forgiveness is an essential component of conflict resolution in a Christian marriage. Holding grudges or resentments can poison a relationship, inhibiting intimacy and hindering spiritual growth. Forgiveness, on the other hand, is a thoughtful and gracious gesture that allows partners to move on from previous hurts and rebuild trust.

Forgiveness is not always easy, especially when one has been seriously injured. It may take time, prayer, and a concentrated effort to overcome the sadness and resentment. However, the advantages of forgiveness are great. When you choose to forgive your spouse, you open the door to healing, reconciliation, and a deeper relationship.

Here are some practical ways to practice forgiveness inside your marriage:

- Recognize the hurt. Don't try to minimize or dismiss your discomfort.

- Pray for your hubby. Ask God to help you forgive and heal your relationship.

- Choose to forgive. Forgiveness is a choice, not a feeling. Make a conscious decision to release your resentments and animosity.

- Communicate your forgiveness. Let your spouse know that you have forgiven them.

- Seek reconciliation. Attempt to rebuild trust and mend your relationship.

Conflict, when handled properly, may strengthen your marriage. It can help you better understand each other, improve your relationship, and build a stronger link. It can also be an opportunity for personal and relational development, imparting valuable lessons about communication, compromise, and forgiveness.

Remember that conflict is not the enemy in marriage; it is how you handle it that is important. By applying biblical principles and practicing healthy communication skills, you can resolve conflicts in an honorable and strengthening manner.

Remember that you're all on the same team during a conflict. You are partners, bound by your love for one another and commitment to your marriage. With God's help and guidance, you may overcome any hurdle and emerge from conflict with a deeper understanding, a stronger bond, and a more resilient love.

Fighting Fair

Conflict, like a fierce summer storm, can flare up abruptly in any marriage. It is the logical outcome of two people with opposing ideals and personalities joining forces to make a life. However, just as a storm can bring much-needed rain or cause catastrophic destruction, fighting can either strengthen or weaken the bonds in your relationship. The goal is to learn how to "fight fair," which entails negotiating disagreements in a way that honors God, respects each other, and, eventually, strengthens your relationship.

Fighting fairly is an art and skill that requires intention, self-awareness, and a commitment to polite communication. It is important to recognize that conflict is about understanding, compromise, and finding solutions that benefit both parties. It is about choosing to participate in disagreements with respect, kindness, and a genuine desire to solve the situation at hand, rather than engaging in harmful behaviors that could ruin the relationship.

One of the most common fallacies in conversations is the tendency to attack the individual rather than the problem. This can include slurs, name-calling, character criticism, or bringing up old grievances. These personal attacks promote defensiveness, intensify conflict, and erode trust. Instead, express your thoughts on the specific matter at hand, using "I" statements to convey your point of view without criticizing or condemning your partner.

Another negative habit is the tendency to generalize or exaggerate. Using phrases like "always" or "never" can leave your spouse feeling constrained and confused. Instead, use specific examples rather than broad generalizations to describe the behavior or situation that is causing you harm.

Another common mistake is to stonewall or withdraw from the debate. This can include withdrawing emotionally, refusing to participate in the discourse, or physically leaving the room. While taking a break can be good when emotions are high, completely withdrawing from the conversation may make your spouse feel abandoned and unheard. Instead, explain your need for a pause openly and courteously, promising your partner that you will resume the conversation once you are both calm.

It is also critical to avoid bringing up previous grievances or other topics. This tactic, known as "kitchen sinking," can derail a conversation and make it difficult to concentrate on the subject at hand. Instead, concentrate on the current problem and resolve it as soon as possible, without bringing up previous hurts or disagreements.

To fight fairly, it is vital to foster an environment of mutual respect and understanding. This includes acknowledging that your partner's point of view is valid, even if you disagree with it. It requires actively listening to people to understand their points of view before defending yours. It requires approaching the conflict with humility and acknowledging that you may not always be accurate.

Here are some practical strategies to handle arguments productively:

- Select the right time and location. Avoid having uncomfortable conversations while weary, stressed, or preoccupied. Find a quiet, secluded space where you can both focus on the conversation without interruptions.

- Begin with prayer. Begin your talk by praying to God for direction, wisdom, and serenity.

- Express your feelings clearly and appropriately. Use "I" statements to express your views without criticizing or condemning your partner.

- Actively listen to your partner's opinions. Pay great attention to their language, nonverbal cues, and emotions. Ask clarifying questions to ensure that you understand their point of view.

- Take turns speaking. Avoid interrupting and speaking over one another. Allow each other to fully express their thoughts and emotions.

- Focus on finding solutions. Collaborate to create mutually acceptable solutions that address both your needs and concerns.

- Be willing to compromise. Recognize that effective dispute resolution typically requires giving and taking. Be willing to meet your partner halfway and find a solution that works for both of you.

- Finish with forgiveness and reconciliation. Get rid of any hate and hatred, and make a concerted effort to go forward. Express your love and loyalty to each other, even if you disagree.

Fighting fair does not imply avoiding confrontation altogether; rather, it entails understanding how to settle problems healthily and constructively. It's about choosing to handle conflict with respect, love, and a genuine desire to strengthen your relationship. By adhering to these recommendations and establishing healthy communication skills, you may turn disagreement from a destructive force into an opportunity for growth, understanding, and a better relationship.

Forgiveness and Reconciliation

Forgiveness in a Christian marriage is more than a polite gesture or sweeping sins under the rug. It is a brave act of love, a deliberate decision to let go of resentment and show grace to your partner, even if they have severely harmed you. It represents God's boundless love and forgiveness for us, recognizing that we are all flawed humans in need of grace and salvation.

The Bible covers forgiveness extensively, emphasizing its significance in mending and restoring relationships. In the Lord's Prayer, Jesus tells us to ask, "Forgive us our debts, as we have forgiven our debtors." This appealing remark underscores the link between accepting God's forgiveness and forgiving others, especially our spouse.

Forgiveness is not a passive act; it is a conscious decision to let go of anger, bitterness, and the desire for vengeance. It is the realization that holding grudges only harms ourselves, polluting our emotions and limiting our ability to love and connect with others.

Forgiveness is essential to a healthy and happy marriage. When disagreements arise, as they inevitably will, forgiveness allows partners to move forward without the burden of past hurts and grudges. It offers the chance for healing, forgiveness, and a renewed sense of connection.

Forgiveness does not involve embracing callous behavior or pretending that nothing terrible has happened. It is about admitting the hurt, letting go of the anger, and choosing to go forward with love and grace. It's about acknowledging that we all make mistakes, fall short, and need forgiveness to experience true freedom and connection in our relationships.

The biblical concept of forgiveness is founded on God's character. He is a God of mercy and compassion, slow to rage and filled with love. He forgives us not because we deserve it, but because He genuinely cares for us. When we choose to forgive our spouses, we are showing the divine quality of compassion and generosity to people who have harmed us.

Forgiveness is not a one-time event; it is an ongoing practice. It may take time, prayer, and a concentrated effort to overcome the sadness and resentment. However, the advantages of forgiveness are great. When you choose to forgive your spouse, you open the door to healing, reconciliation, and a deeper relationship.

Here are some practical tips to assist you in negotiating the process of forgiveness and reconciliation in your marriage.

Recognize the hurt. Don't try to minimize or dismiss your discomfort. Allow yourself to grieve the hurt and acknowledge its influence on you.

Pray for your hubby. Ask God to help you forgive and heal your relationship. Pray for understanding, compassion, and the capacity to let go of hostility.

Choose to forgive. Forgiveness is a choice, not a feeling. Make a conscious decision to let go of the resentment and bitterness you are harboring.

Communicate your forgiveness. Let your spouse know that you have forgiven them. This might be a helpful step towards reconciliation and healing.

Seek reconciliation. Attempt to rebuild trust and mend your relationship. This could entail apologizing for your role in the conflict, listening to your spouse's point of view, and making amends if possible.

Remember that forgiveness is a journey. It may take time to fully forgive and reconcile. Be patient with yourself and your partner, and continue to pray for God's guidance and healing.

Here are a few practices to help you practice forgiveness and reconciliation in your marriage.

Write a letter of forgiveness. Express your hurt, anger, and willingness to forgive. This might help you understand your emotions and forgive your partner.

Pray together for healing. Ask God to help you forgive one another and repair your friendship.

Make a list of the characteristics you admire in your spouse. This may help you focus on the positive aspects of your relationship and cultivate a sense of gratitude.

Plan a special date night or activity together. This can help to reconnect and rebuild intimacy after a fight.

Seek counseling if necessary. If you're having problems forgiving or reconciling, consider seeking professional assistance from a Christian counselor or therapist.

Forgiveness does not indicate weakness; rather, it demonstrates strength and courage. It is a choice to move on from the past and embrace the future, to let go of resentment and accept love. It exemplifies God's grace and mercy, revealing the power of His love to heal and reestablish shattered relationships.

As you practice forgiveness and reconciliation in your marriage, you will understand that it is more than just letting go of the past; it is about creating a future full of hope, healing, and a deeper connection than ever before.

<u>**Key Points**</u>

→ Conflict is an inescapable part of any marriage, but it can also be an opportunity for growth and deeper connection if handled correctly.

→ Using biblical conflict resolution themes such as forgiveness, kindness, and patience will help you manage disagreements in a healthy and God-honoring way.

→ "Fighting fair" requires establishing ground rules for debates, avoiding destructive inclinations, and seeking mutually acceptable solutions.

→ Forgiveness is essential for mending and repairing relationships following a disagreement. To let go of resentment and demonstrate grace, one must make a conscious decision.

→ Reconciliation is the process of reestablishing trust and connection after a quarrel. It involves communication, empathy, and a willingness to make amends.

<u>**Self-Reflection Questions**</u>

1. How do you normally handle disagreements in your marriage? Do you like to avoid it, confront it in front of, or somewhere in the middle?

____

____

____

____

____

2. What damaging tendencies have you identified in your conflict resolution style? How can you address these behaviors while "fighting fair" with your spouse?

____

____

____

____

____

3. How easily do you forgive your lover for hurting you? What are some barriers to your ability to forgive?

____

____

____

____

____

4. How do you generally approach reconciliation after a conflict? How can you improve your approach to reconciliation?

____

____

____

____

5. How has constructive conflict enhanced your marriage and relationship with your spouse?

____

____

____

Chapter 5: Love Languages

"Love is patient, love is kind. It does not envy, it does not boast, it is not proud. It does not dishonor others, it is not self-seeking, it is not easily angered, it keeps no record of wrongs. Love does not delight in evil but rejoices with the truth. It always protects, always trusts, always hopes, always perseveres." -
1 Corinthians 13:4-7

Love, in its countless manifestations, is the very essence of a happy marriage, the invisible thread that unites two hearts. It is the language that speaks louder than words, the glue that holds two people together, the foundation for a lifetime of shared experiences and mutual improvement.

In a Christian marriage, love has a deeper meaning. It's not just a fleeting emotion or a romantic ideal; it's a reflection of God's love, a selfless, sacrificial, and unconditional commitment to the well-being of others. It is a choice to put your spouse's needs ahead of your own, to freely offer grace and forgiveness, and to love them through thick and thin.

Understanding how you and your spouse express and experience love is essential for building a strong and fulfilling relationship. Here is where the concept of love languages comes into play. Dr. Gary Chapman identified love languages, which are the unique ways we give and receive love. They are the love dialects, the specific sentences that most clearly address our emotions.

The five major love languages are:

- Affirmation is the act of expressing love through spoken or written words of thanks, encouragement, and compassion.

- Acts of Service: Showing your love by doing things for your partner, such as completing chores, running errands, or offering practical help.

- Receiving presents: Feeling valued through tangible expressions of affection, such as thoughtful presents, tokens of appreciation, or simple acts of kindness.

- Quality time is spent feeling love via undivided attention, meaningful conversations, and collaborative activities.

- Physical contact is defined as feeling loved via physical expressions of affection such as hugs, kisses, handholding, and cuddling.

Each person has a primary love language that speaks most strongly to their heart. When you learn to communicate in your spouse's love language, you replenish their emotional love tank and start a positive feedback cycle of love and appreciation.

Discovering your own and your spouse's love languages can be illuminating, showing a deeper degree of connection and understanding in your marriage. It can help you understand why certain expressions of love are more meaningful to you than others, as well as how to express your love to your spouse in a way that they will actually enjoy and appreciate.

Understanding love languages can also help you resolve conflicts and misunderstandings in your marriage. Recognizing that your partner may express and experience love in different ways than you do encourages you to approach disagreements with more respect and compassion. You can avoid taking their actions or words personally by focusing on their true intentions and aspirations.

For example, if your spouse's primary love language is Acts of Service, they may feel most loved when you assist them with housework or practical support. If Words of Affirmation are your major love language, you may feel the most loved when your partner expresses their appreciation and affection. If you are unaware of these distinctions, you may misinterpret your spouse's actions or words, resulting in resentment and hostility.

Learning to speak your spouse's love language is an act of love that demonstrates your sincere concern for their wants and desires. It indicates your respect and appreciation for them, as well as your desire to make them feel loved and valued.

Here are some practical ways to communicate your spouse's love language:

- Pay attention to how they show their affection for you. This might provide you with some insight into their love language.

- Observe how children respond to varied displays of love. Consider what makes them feel the most loved and valued.

- Ask them directly about their love language. Talk frankly and honestly about how you give and receive love.

- Make a conscious effort to express affection in their favorite language. This may force you to step out of your comfort zone and try new things.

- Express your affection in a creative and purposeful manner. Find unique and meaningful ways to show your spouse how much you care.

- Don't be afraid to ask for what you need. Tell your lover what makes you feel the most loved.

Speaking your spouse's love language does not mean persuading or pressuring them to do what you want. It's about genuinely expressing love in a way that touches their heart. It is about making them feel seen, heard, and valued.

When you learn how to speak in your spouse's love language, you start a positive cycle of love and appreciation in your marriage. You strengthen and deepen your link, resulting in a more fulfilling and enjoyable relationship.

Love languages are more than just a tool for improving your relationships; they express God's love for us. God speaks to us in a variety of ways, including through His Word, creation, the Holy Spirit, and the love and support of others. He understands our individual needs and desires, and He expresses His love in ways that touch our hearts.

Learning to speak your spouse's love language not only strengthens your marriage but also reflects God's love for them. You are teaching children that they are valued, beloved, and passionately loved in the same way that God loves them.

Love languages are a powerful tool for building a strong and joyful Christian marriage. They help you understand how you and your spouse give and receive love, and they teach you how to express love in a way that strikes your heart. As you learn to speak your spouse's love language, you begin a positive cycle of love and appreciation that strengthens and deepens your bond.

Discovering Your Partner's Love Language

Understanding the complexities of how each partner gives and receives affection is essential in the complicated dance of love and marriage, in which two individuals join forces to create a life. The concept of "love languages" illuminates the path to deeper connection and mutual fulfillment.

Dr. Gary Chapman defined love languages as the specific ways in which people express and experience love. They are the love dialects, the specific sentences that most clearly address our emotions. Love languages, like spoken languages, differ between cultures, influencing how we perceive love and respect.

The five major love languages are:

- Words of Affirmation: For some people, making vocal expressions of love, appreciation, and encouragement is the most effective way to feel valued. Hearing "I love you," receiving compliments, or reading a nice note can all help them refill their emotional love tank.

- Acts of Service: Other people feel most loved when their spouse takes the initiative to meet their needs or reduce their burden. Chores, errands, and practical assistance are all acts of love that they greatly value.

- Receiving Gifts: Tangible demonstrations of affection can make someone feel cherished. Thoughtful gifts, gestures of appreciation, or small acts of kindness express care and consideration in ways that words cannot.

- Quality Time: For many people, undivided attention and shared experiences are the most powerful signs of love. Spending time together, having meaningful conversations, and creating shared memories are the keys to their hearts.

- Physical Touch: Hugs, kisses, handholding, and snuggling are some of the most common ways that individuals feel loved and connected. These bodily movements convey warmth, security, and genuine devotion.

Each person has a primary love language, a dialect that speaks most directly to their inner core. Learning to speak your partner's love language allows you to effectively communicate love in a way that they understand and cherish. You are filling their emotional love tank, making them feel appreciated, valued, and intimately linked.

Discovering your own and your partner's love languages may be a transformative experience, revealing new levels of intimacy and understanding in your marriage. It can help you understand why certain expressions of love are more meaningful to you than others, as well as how to express love to your partner in a way that they will truly receive and appreciate.

Consider taking the self-assessment exam below to determine your love language and that of your spouse. For each question, choose the option (a, b, or c) that best expresses your desire or your opinion of your partner's preference.

1. Which of the following would make you feel the most loved and appreciated by your partner?

a) Hearing the words "I love you" or "I appreciate you."
b) Ask them to assist you with a chore or task.
c) Getting a thoughtful gift from someone.

2. Which of the following would make you feel the most connected with your partner?

a) Spending valuable time together, talking and sharing experiences.
b) Allowing them to physically express affection by hugging or kissing you.
c) Receiving a small gesture of goodwill from them, such as a note or a cup of coffee.

3. Which of the following would make you feel most valued by your partner?

a) Requesting that they do something special for you, such as planning a surprise date or preparing your favorite food.
b) Being encouraged and supported by others.
c) Having people pay you full attention while you speak.

4. Which of the following would make you feel more understood by your partner?

a) Asking them to pay close attention while you communicate your views and feelings.
b) Allowing them to express their feelings for you through physical touch.
c) Receiving a gift from them that shows they were thinking about you.

5. Which of the following would make you feel most appreciated by your partner?

a) Encouraging them to spend meaningful time with you despite their busy schedules.
b) Requesting that someone do anything to make your life easier, such as do a chore or run an errand.
c) Receiving a heartfelt note or letter from them, expressing love and gratitude.

Scoring:

- Mostly a's: Your primary love language is usually words of affirmation.
- Mostly b's: Your primary love language is likely actions of service.
- Mostly c's: Receiving Gifts is your primary love language.

If your replies were more evenly distributed, you may have a second love language or be receptive to many love languages.

Remember that this self-evaluation is only the beginning. The most important thing is to be open and honest with your partner about how you both give and receive love. Share your results and discuss what makes you feel the most loved and appreciated.

Understanding love languages is not about categorizing people or limiting their romantic careers. It's about getting to know yourself and your spouse better so you may show your love in a way that touches their heart. It's about creating a more fulfilling and joyful relationship in which you both feel respected, cherished, and deeply connected.

Speaking Each Other's Language

In the symphony of love that is marriage, each partner plays a unique instrument, contributing their melody to the lovely total. Understanding your partner's love language is analogous to studying the notes they play or the specific songs that have the most emotional resonance with them. When you speak their love language, you create a magnificent duet, a harmonious expression of love and admiration that strengthens and improves your connection.

Speaking your partner's love language is not about manipulating or pushing them to do what you want; rather, it is about honestly expressing love in a way they understand and appreciate. It is about making them feel seen, heard, and valued, which will fill their emotional love tank and create a positive feedback loop of affection and connection.

If your partner's dominant love language is Words of Affirmation, they thrive on verbal expressions of affection, admiration, and encouragement. **Here are several approaches to communicating in their language:**

- Offer sincere compliments. Observe what they do well and express your admiration for their abilities, skills, and character.

- Express gratitude for their contributions. Tell them how much you appreciate their efforts, big or small.

- Send them positive notes or emails. A simple message of love and support can boost their morale and make them feel important.

- Write them a heartfelt letter or card. Take the time to express your feelings in a practical way that they will appreciate.

- Tell them how much you love and appreciate them. Do not assume they understand; instead, express your feelings directly and repeatedly.

If your partner's major love language is Acts of Service, they will be most grateful when you take steps to meet their needs or lighten their load. **Here are several approaches to communicating in their language:**

- Assist with domestic duties. Offer to do the dishes, laundry, and yard work.

- Run errands for them. Collect groceries, dry cleaning, and medications.

- Offer to help with a project. If they're working on a difficult task, offer your assistance and support.

- Take care of whatever they had intended to undertake. Fix the leaky faucet, organize the packed closet, or complete that unfinished task.

- Surprise them with a completed chore. Imagine how happy they will be when they return home to a spotless house or a freshly trimmed lawn.

If Receiving Gifts is your partner's primary love language, physical expressions of affection will make them feel appreciated. **Here are several approaches to communicating in their language:**

- Give them meaningful gifts. Choose gifts that reflect their interests, hobbies, or personality.

- Bring them tiny expressions of gratitude. A single flower, a favorite candy bar, or a small present can express your love and attentiveness.

- Surprise them with a random present. A surprise gift could be an excellent way to show your caring.

- Create a handcrafted gift. A personalized gift, such as a framed photo or a hand-knitted scarf, shows that you took the time and effort to convey your love.

- Give the gift of your time. Offer to spend the afternoon doing something they enjoy, even if it is not your preferred activity.

If your partner's primary love language is Quality Time, they desire your undivided attention and shared experiences. **Here are several approaches to communicating in their language:**

- Plan a unique date night. Set aside time to communicate with your partner without interruption.

- Engage in meaningful conversations. Listen closely, ask questions, and communicate your thoughts and feelings.

- Create shared experiences. Take a walk, attend a concert, or try a new pastime together.

- Make time for daily connections. Even a few minutes of focused discussion per day can make a difference.

- Set aside your phone and other distractions. When you spend time with your lover, offer him or her your full attention.

If your partner's primary love language is physical touch, they will feel most appreciated through physical demonstrations of affection. **Here are several approaches to communicating in their language:**

- Offer hugs, kisses, and cuddles. Physical contact can convey warmth, security, and a deep devotion.

- Hold hands while walking or sitting together. This simple action can create a sense of connection and closeness.

- Give them a back rub or massage. Physical touch may be both relaxing and healing, indicating concern for their well-being.

- Cuddle up on the couch and enjoy a movie. Physical contact can bring comfort and security.

- Give them an unexpected hug or kiss. An unexpected display of affection may improve their day and make them feel valued.

Speaking your partner's love language is a continual practice, a constant expression of love and gratitude that strengthens and enhances your connection. It's about being purposeful in your actions, paying attention to your partner's needs and desires, and devising new ways to demonstrate how much you care.

As you learn to speak your partner's love language, you'll understand that it's not just about filling their emotional love tank, but also yours. When you see your partner's face light up with pleasure and thanks, your heart feels warm and content. You get excited about giving love in a way that is significant to them, and you strengthen your bond in the process.

Speaking each other's love language is a beautiful dance, a happy exchange of passion and praise that enhances your marriage and promotes a deeper sense of connection. It's a moment to celebrate your love, show your gratitude, and reinforce the sacred bond you have as husband and wife.

Key Points

→ Understanding your partner's love language allows you to communicate love in a way that they will fully comprehend and enjoy.

→ Words of encouragement, acts of service, getting presents, spending quality time together, and physical touch are the five love languages.

→ Each person has a primary love language that speaks most strongly to their heart.

→ Learning to speak your partner's love language strengthens your bond, deepens your connection, and results in a more fulfilling relationship.

→ Speaking your partner's love language is an act of love that demonstrates your sincere concern for their needs and desires.

Self-Reflection Questions

1. What is your primary love language? What makes you feel most loved and appreciated?

____

____

____

____

2. What do you think is your partner's primary love language? What have you noticed about their preferences and how they express love for you?

____

____

____

3. How often do you actively express your love for your partner using their love language? What specific steps can you take to speak their language more often?

4. How well do you understand your partner's need for love and affection? Are you meeting their needs in a way that appeals to them?

5. How can you use the concept of love languages to improve communication and resolve conflict in your marriage?

Chapter 6: Intimacy: Beyond the Physical

"And the two will become one flesh.' So they are no longer two but one flesh. Therefore what God has joined together, let no one separate." - Mark 10:8-9

In the context of a Christian marriage, intimacy is a multifaceted diamond that displays the brilliance of a strong and enduring bond. It is more than just physical contact; it is an emotional, spiritual, and intellectual bond between two souls, a holy union in which vulnerability is encouraged, trust is cultivated, and love grows.

Intimacy is a safe place where you can be yourself, without pretenses or masks. It's a place where you may communicate your hopes and dreams, as well as your fears and insecurities, knowing that you'll be met with love and acceptance. It is the link that binds you together during life's storms, the anchor that keeps you grounded in the face of change and uncertainty.

Emotional connection is the cornerstone of a happy and fulfilling marriage. It is the ability to connect deeply and truly with your partner, communicate your innermost thoughts, and feel entirely understood and cherished. It is about creating a safe space where you can be vulnerable and openly express your emotions without fear of being judged or rejected.

Emotional intimacy requires a willingness to open up your heart to your spouse and communicate your ideas and feelings, even if they are difficult or painful to express. It necessitates active listening, a genuine desire to understand your spouse's point of view, and empathy for their situation.

When you cultivate emotional intimacy in your marriage, you create a connection that goes beyond the surface level. You build a foundation of trust and understanding, allowing you to face life's challenges together. You create an environment in which you may grow and thrive, knowing that your spouse knows and accepts you for who you are.

Spiritual intimacy is an important part of connection in Christian marriages. It is the shared journey of faith, the intertwining of your spiritual life as you seek God together. It is about praying together, studying Scripture, worshiping God as a couple, and supporting one another's spiritual development.

Spiritual intimacy promotes a sense of togetherness and purpose inside your marriage. It connects your heart to God's, guiding you toward a shared goal for your life and relationships. It offers courage and comfort during difficult times, reminding you that you are not alone on your journey.

When you cultivate spiritual intimacy in your marriage, you create a sacred space where you can connect with God and each other on a deeper level. You create the groundwork for your relationship by creating a shared faith that provides meaning and purpose.

Intellectual intimacy is the connection of minds, and the sharing of ideas, attitudes, and viewpoints. It is about having stimulating conversations, learning from one another, and encouraging one another to grow intellectually. It is about acknowledging each other's unique perspectives and finding common ground in your intellectual pursuits.

Intellectual intimacy can spark excitement and wonder in your marriage. It can help keep your presentations fresh and entertaining, preventing them from becoming dull or predictable. It can also help you mature as individuals and couples by widening your perspectives and improving your grasp of the world around you.

Physical intimacy is important in marriage, but it is simply one part of the multifaceted jewel of intimacy. Physical touch shows love and affection, while the sharing of pleasure and proximity strengthens the bond between husband and wife.

Physical intimacy is a gift from God, a precious act to be shared and enjoyed in the married bond. It is a way to express love, connect, and experience the fullness of God's plan for marriage.

Physical closeness becomes much more important and satisfying when it is accompanied by emotional, spiritual, and intellectual bonds. It shows a deep and abiding love while also celebrating your unique relationship as husband and wife.

Nurturing intimacy on all levels is essential for a thriving and fulfilling marriage. It takes intention, effort, and a willingness to be vulnerable and open with your spouse. It includes providing a safe space in which you can be yourself and share your hearts and minds without fear of being judged or rejected.

Here are some practical strategies to create a connection inside your marriage:

- Prioritize communication. Make time for meaningful conversations where you may share your thoughts, opinions, and experiences.

- Practice active listening. Pay attention to your spouse's words, nonverbal cues, and emotions. Seek to understand their point of view and empathize with their situation.

- Show your respect and admiration on a regular basis. Tell your spouse how much you appreciate and cherish them.

- Spend quality time together. Set aside time for shared activities, date nights, and uninterrupted connection.

- Pray together. Seek out God's counsel and presence in your relationships.

- Study the Bible together. Develop your faith and understanding of God's marriage plan.

- Support each other's dreams and goals. Encourage one another to grow and pursue your passions.

- Display physical affection. Touch, hugs, kisses, and intimacy are all ways to express affection.

- Forgive each other kindly. Let go of past wounds and resentments.

- Seek expert assistance if necessary. If you are having difficulty with intimacy, do not be hesitant to seek help from a Christian counselor or therapist.

Intimacy is a journey, a continuous process of development and discovery. It's about providing a secure environment in which you can be yourself, connect on a deep and meaningful level, and let your love flourish. It's about weaving your life together, thread by thread, into a tapestry of shared experiences, mutual support, and unwavering love.

Emotional Intimacy

Emotional intimacy is the foundation of a deeply connected and fulfilling marriage. It's the safe harbor where hearts meet, where vulnerabilities can be revealed without fear of being judged, and where the most intimate aspects of yourself are embraced and appreciated. It serves as the foundation for trust, allowing love to thrive and weather life's storms.

Emotional intimacy is not a destination; it is a journey in which you open your heart to your spouse, share your inner world, and allow them to fully know you. It's about creating an environment in which you can be real, openly express your feelings, and feel safe enough to be vulnerable without fear of rejection.

Vulnerability is the foundation of emotional connection. It is the willingness to let your guard down and reveal your true self, with all of its flaws and fears, to your spouse. It's about sharing your concerns, dreams, goals, and pain, knowing that you'll be received with love and acceptance.

Vulnerability is not weakness; it is courage. It takes courage to open your heart and reveal your darkest worries and doubts to another person. However, choosing vulnerability opens up the possibility of deep connection and intimacy. You let your spouse see the real you, the person behind the mask, and they love you even more for it.

Trust is the basis on which vulnerability can grow. It is the assumption that your partner will protect your heart and treat your vulnerabilities with care and respect. It is the belief that you can express your darkest worries and insecurities without fear of being judged or betrayed.

Building trust requires time and persistence. It's acquired by consistent acts of love, devotion, and support. It is strengthened by open communication, honesty, and the courage to be vulnerable with one another.

When you establish trust in your marriage, you create a safe environment in which emotional intimacy can flourish. You let yourselves be fully seen and known by one another without fear of rejection or judgment. You form an unbreakable link, a foundation that can survive the storms of life.

Shared experiences are the foundation of emotional connection. They are the moments that connect your life, resulting in a common history and a better understanding of one another. Whether it's a romantic getaway, a difficult battle, or just a regular day spent together, shared experiences form a bond that is unique and priceless.

When you consciously plan shared events with your partner, you are investing in your emotional bond. You're creating a reservoir of memories, inside jokes, and shared understanding to help you get through life's ups and downs. You're forming a bond that will be difficult to break, one that will become stronger with time.

To foster emotional connection in your marriage, try the following exercises and questions:

- Share your "inner world" with one another. Take turns expressing your thoughts, emotions, dreams, and anxieties. Listen attentively and without passing judgment.

- Practice being vulnerable. Share something with your partner that you've never told anybody else. This could be a worry, an insecurity, or a past injury.

- Express thankfulness for one another. Spend time appreciating your spouse's characteristics and thanking them for being in your life.

- Reflect on common experiences. Discuss your favorite memories together, whether big or small. Remember the times when you were happy, laughing, and feeling connected.

- Schedule a special date night or activity. Create new shared experiences that enhance your friendship and leave enduring memories.

- Ask each other open-ended questions. Ask questions that promote deeper conversation and self-reflection.

- Practice forgiveness. Let go of any old hurts and resentments that may be impeding your emotional connection.

- Pray together. Seek God's counsel and presence in your relationship, and ask Him to help you develop an emotional connection.

Emotional connection is not a luxury; it is essential for a healthy Christian marriage. It is the basis upon which trust, vulnerability, and love can grow. It's the safe harbor where you can be yourself, connect on a deep and meaningful level, and your love can endure life's storms.

As you build emotional intimacy in your marriage, you'll realize that it's more than just discussing your emotions; it's about creating a space for you to both grow, heal, and experience the fullness of God's purpose for love and connection.

Spiritual Intimacy

In the realm of Christian marriage, where two lives are united with God's blessing, spiritual intimacy serves as a guiding star, illuminating the path to a meaningful and permanent bond. It is the sacred zone where hearts connect not only with one another but also with the divine, forging a bond that transcends the earthly realm and anchors the relationship in eternal truths.

Spiritual intimacy is the lifeblood of a God-centered marriage, feeding and strengthening the tie between husband and wife. It is the shared pursuit of God's presence, the desire to grow in faith and understanding, and an unwavering commitment to journey together down the path of righteousness.

When couples prioritize spiritual intimacy, they invite God to be the cornerstone of their relationship, illuminating their path and strengthening their bonds. They understand that their marriage is more than just a human contract; it is a valuable relationship sanctified by God and designed to reflect His love and purpose.

Spiritual intimacy entails more than simply attending church together or praying before meals; it entails developing a deep and lasting relationship with God as individuals and as a marriage. It is about seeking His presence in all elements of your life, from the mundane to the significant. It is about allowing His Word to shape your thoughts, attitudes, and actions.

Shared prayer is an essential part of spiritual connection. When couples pray together, they create a sacred space where they can express their gratitude, concerns, and hopes. They keep God at the center of their relationship, seeking His guidance, wisdom, and strength.

Praying together can take many shapes, from spontaneous chats with God to more structured prayers of adoration, confession, and intercession. The goal is to make prayer a regular and necessary part of your daily routine, as a natural expression of your reliance on God and desire to walk beside Him.

Consider establishing a time to pray together every day, whether it's first thing in the morning, before bed, or during a family meal. Try out different prayer methods, such as taking turns praying openly, praying silently together, or keeping a prayer journal to record your wishes and thoughts.

Worship is another powerful way to increase spiritual connectedness. Couples worship together, raising their voices and emotions in praise and love of God. They celebrate His goodness, constancy, and love. They sacrifice their particular wills for His greater purpose, uniting their hearts with His.

Find opportunities to worship together, such as attending church services, listening to worship music at home, or participating in online worship gatherings. Allow your heart to be moved by God's music, message, and presence. Share your thoughts and feelings about the experience later to enhance your friendship through shared reflection.

Service is the external manifestation of a spiritual relationship. When couples serve together, they put their faith into action by combining their abilities and talents to help others and make a difference in the world. They demonstrate their love for God by loving their neighbors and showing compassion and generosity to those in need.

Look for ways to serve together in your community, such as volunteering at a local charity, attending a mission trip, or simply supporting a neighbor in need. After that, discuss your experiences and perspectives, concentrating on how serving others has influenced your religion and relationships.

Exploring your faith together is an essential part of spiritual intimacy. It's about asking questions, receiving responses, and engaging in meaningful debates about your beliefs and values. It is about learning from one another, pushing one another, and growing together in your understanding of God and His Word.

Read books and articles about faith, attend seminars and conferences, or join a small group for discussion and friendship. Create a safe space where you may express your thoughts and feelings without fear of being judged or rejected. Encourage one another to ask questions, seek answers, and deepen your understanding of God's truth.

Supporting each other's spiritual development is essential for maintaining a healthy and dynamic spiritual connection in your marriage. It is about encouraging one another to pursue a deeper connection with God, develop spiritual disciplines, and live out your faith in everyday life.

Pray for one other's spiritual growth, go to church together, and encourage one another to participate in Bible studies or small groups. Create an environment in which both of you can develop spiritually, encouraging one other's different paths and celebrating each other's triumphs.

Spiritual connection is a dynamic and ever-changing experience. Developing your faith together requires intention, work, and commitment. It's about seeking God's presence in all areas of your life and allowing His Word to influence your thoughts, attitudes, and actions.

When you prioritize spiritual intimacy in your marriage, you will discover that it is not only about strengthening your bond with one another but also about increasing your connection with God. Your relationship will be more peaceful, joyful, and purposeful. You will discover strength and comfort throughout difficult circumstances. Furthermore, you will leave a legacy of faith and love for future generations.

Key Points

- Intimacy in marriage is more than just physical connection. It includes emotional, spiritual, and intellectual connections.

- Emotional intimacy requires vulnerability, trust, and open communication about thoughts and feelings.

- Spiritual intimacy is the mutual desire for God's presence in your marriage, which includes praying, worshiping, and serving together.

- Intellectual intimacy requires engaging on an intellectual level, discussing ideas, and challenging one another's perspectives.

- Nurturing intimacy on all levels is essential for a thriving and fulfilling marriage.

<u>Self-Reflection Questions</u>

1. How would you describe your marriage's emotional intimacy? Do you feel safe and comfortable sharing your most sensitive thoughts and feelings with your spouse?

____

____

____

____

2. How do you and your partner develop a spiritual connection in your marriage? What are some ways to strengthen your connection with God, both personally and as a couple?

____

____

____

____

3. How do you communicate intellectually with your spouse? Do you engage in stimulating talks and share interests or ideas?

____

____

____

____

4. How do you prioritize and sustain physical intimacy in your marriage? Is it an expression of a deeper emotional and spiritual connection?

____

____

____

____

____

5. What specific steps can you take in your marriage to promote intimacy on all levels?

____

____

____

____

____

Chapter 7: Shared Goals and Dreams

"Two are better than one, because they have a good return for their labor: If either of them falls down, one can help the other up. But pity anyone who falls and has no one to help them up." - Ecclesiastes 4:9-10

A strong and vibrant marriage is more than just a shared present; it is a shared future, woven from the threads of similar goals, mutual aspirations, and a common vision for a life together. When couples dream together, they create a roadmap for their journey, a sense of purpose and direction that guides their actions and strengthens their connection.

Shared goals and objectives are the foundation for a common future. They are the ideals that unite two hearts and serve as the foundation for a couple's meaningful and purposeful lives. When couples build a vision for their future, they instill excitement and anticipation, as well as a shared objective that fuels their loyalty and drive.

In a Christian marriage, shared goals and desires take on spiritual meaning. They become an expression of faith, embracing God's purpose for their lives and relationships, as well as a desire to align their aims with His plan. This unified vision displays their faith in God's guidance and commitment to building a future that glorifies Him.

Creating a shared vision for your future takes more than just picking where to live or how many children to have; it requires connecting your hearts and brains, values and priorities, and individual aspirations to a common purpose. It is about creating a road map for your journey together, deciding where you want to go and how you plan to get there.

This process of vision casting requires open and honest communication, a willingness to listen to each other's aims and aspirations, and a desire to find common ground. It is about respecting each other's differences but also recognizing the need to create a shared vision that reflects both your desires and values.

Here are some questions to help you navigate the vision casting process.

What are your dreams and goals? What are you enthusiastic about? What do you want to achieve in your life?

____

____

____

What are your marriage dreams and goals? What type of life do you plan to have together? What values and priorities would you like to establish for your relationship?

____

____

____

What are your spiritual goals for your marriage? How do you want to grow in your religion together? How do you hope to serve God and make a difference in the world?

____

____

____

What are your financial goals for the marriage? How do you hope to manage your money and reach financial stability?

____

____

____

What are your family goals for your marriage? Do you want to have children? How would you want to raise them?

____

____

____

What are your ambitions for your marriage? How do you aim to support one another's personal growth and development?

____

____

____

After you've stated your common goals and dreams, you should design a plan to achieve them. This may entail setting specific milestones, creating a calendar, or identifying resources and support systems to help you along the way. It's also critical to examine your vision regularly, making adjustments as needed and acknowledging your progress along the way.

Creating a shared vision for your future requires ongoing communication, flexibility, and a willingness to adapt to changing circumstances. It's about keeping your eyes on the prize, collaborating to achieve your mutual goals, and encouraging one another every step of the way.

Supporting one another's ambitions is essential for personal growth and marital happiness. It is about creating a safe and accepting environment in which both partners feel encouraged to pursue their passions, develop their talents, and realize their full potential.

This aid can take many forms, including words of encouragement and celebration of accomplishments, as well as actual assistance and problem-solving. It's about being there in your partner's journey, listening to their dreams and worries, and creating a safe space for them to admit their flaws while also celebrating their successes.

Here are some practical ways to support each other's goals:

- Communicate plainly and honestly about your personal goals and objectives. Share your enthusiasm, concerns, and progress. Listen to your partner's aspirations and offer encouragement and support.

- Celebrate each other's accomplishments, big and small. Recognize their efforts, appreciate their victories, and express your satisfaction with their progress.

- Offer practical assistance and support. Help them overcome obstacles, develop solutions, and connect with resources that will help them achieve their goals.

- Create a space for personal development. Encourage your mate to pursue their hobbies, interests, and educational ambitions. Offer to take on additional chores to free up their time.

- Show patience and understanding. Personal development involves time and effort. Be patient as your partner improves and offer encouragement along the road.

- Respect each other's originality. Recognize that your partner's dreams and goals may differ from your own. Encourage and celebrate their originality.

- Pray for each other's development and success. Ask God to guide and empower your partner in their attempts.

- Offer encouragement and motivation. Remind your companion of their qualities and potential. Believe in them, even if they question themselves.

Supporting one another's aims should not involve pressuring your spouse to fulfill your own goals or expectations. It's all about creating a safe and supportive environment in which they can explore their interests, pursue their own goals, and become the best versions of themselves.

When you prioritize mutual support in your marriage, you create a dynamic synergy in which both partners are motivated to grow and prosper. This mutual progress develops and deepens the tie, resulting in a more fulfilling and active partnership.

Shared goals and desires act as a compass, directing a marriage toward a fulfilling future. They form the basis for a couple's legacy of love, purpose, and mutual success. When couples dream together, they create a road map for their trip, a shared objective that fuels their passion and strengthens their love.

Vision Casting for Your Future

A shared vision for the future acts as a compass for marriage, a North Star that guides a pair through life's storms and currents. It's the image you create of the life you want to live, the objectives you want to attain, and the legacy you want to leave behind.

Couples who engage in vision casting are doing more than just creating plans; they are weaving their hopes and dreams together to form a shared tapestry of aspirations and goals. They're connecting their hearts and minds, charting a common course for their journey, and strengthening their bond.

This shared vision is not a static image; it is a living, breathing organism that transforms and evolves as you grow together. It inspires, motivates, and brings you together, reminding you of your goals and the significance of your connection.

Honest and honest communication is essential for building a shared vision. It's about finding time to dream together, discussing your unique goals and objectives, and paying close attention to your partner's desires. It's about finding common ground, identifying shared goals, and integrating your ambitions into a cohesive vision for the future.

The act of sharing and listening is a show of love and respect. It's a way to honor each other's distinct characteristics while also recognizing the importance of unity and shared purpose in your marriage. It's about establishing an environment in which you may feel heard, appreciated, and supported in your goals.

As you start to express your vision, think about the following characteristics of your life together:

Spiritual Development: How do you envision your religious journey progressing individually and as a couple? What spiritual goals do you want to achieve together? How can you support one another's spiritual growth and development?

____

____

____

Family Life: What kind of family would you like to have? How many children would you like to have, if any? Which values and traditions do you want to pass down to your children?

____

____

____

Career and finance: What are your professional goals? How do you envision your financial future? How can you support each other to reach their professional goals while simultaneously maintaining your family's financial security?

____

____

____

Personal Growth: What personal goals do you have for yourself? How can you encourage and support one another while you follow your passions and interests?

____

____

____

Community Involvement: How do you aim to help your community? Which causes or organizations are you most passionate about? How can you work together to positively impact the world around you?

____

____

____

Travel and Leisure: What are your travel dreams? What hobbies or activities do you enjoy doing together? How can you live a life that is enjoyable, leisurely, and adventurous?

____

____

____

Once you've set your personal and group goals, it's time to start combining them into a shared vision for the future. This includes recognizing common ground, prioritizing your goals, and developing a plan to achieve them.

Here are some exercises and prompts to help you describe your vision and create a plan:

- Create a vision board by collecting photographs, quotes, and statements that represent your ambitions and goals. This can be a fun and creative way to make your idea a reality while still keeping it in mind.

- Goal Setting Worksheet: Create a worksheet that details your specific short- and long-term goals. Break down each goal into smaller, more manageable tasks and set a deadline for accomplishing them.

- Values Clarification Exercise: Discuss your basic values and how they connect to your long-term goals. This may help you ensure that your goals and aspirations are in line with your basic concepts and values.

- Strengths and Limitations Assessment: Discuss how you can help each other reach your common vision, as well as your unique strengths and limits. This allows you to use your strengths and encourage one another in areas where you may develop.

- Accountability Partner: Assign a trustworthy friend or mentor to be your accountability partner, someone who will encourage, support, and hold you accountable to your objectives.

Creating a shared vision is an ongoing process that requires regular discussion, evaluation, and adjustments along the way. Your vision may change as you progress individually and as a pair. The key is to keep focused on your mutual goals, promote one another's desires, and enjoy your accomplishments along the road.

A shared vision is a powerful force in a marriage. It promotes a sense of community, purpose, and direction. It strengthens your bond, deepens your connection, and inspires you to work toward a common goal. It serves as a reminder that you are more than just two people living their lives together; you are a team, a collaboration, and a constructive force in the world.

Keep God at the heart of your shared vision for the future. Seek His guidance, understanding, and strength. Align your dreams with His plan for your life. And trust that He will lead you down a path of love, joy, and fulfillment.

Supporting Each Other's Aspirations

A strong and vibrant marriage is like a garden with two individual flowers blooming side by side, each with its distinct beauty and aroma. Just as each flower requires special care and attention to grow, each spouse in a marriage requires support and encouragement to pursue their own particular goals and desires. This reciprocal support creates a fruitful environment for both partners to grow, flourish, and reach their greatest potential.

In the framework of a Christian marriage, supporting each other's aims has a deeper meaning. It recognizes that God has personally gifted each person and that those gifts are meant to be used for His glory and the benefit of the world. When couples encourage and empower each other's personal growth and development, they are effectively collaborating with God to carry out His purpose for their lives.

Supporting your spouse's aspirations is a sign of love, indicating that you value their aims and believe in their talents. It's an opportunity to demonstrate that you're more than just their life partner; you're also their biggest cheerleader, confidante, and unwavering supporter.

This support can take many forms, ranging from words of encouragement and celebration of their triumphs to practical assistance and help in overcoming obstacles. It's about being there in their journey, listening to their hopes and concerns, and creating a safe space for them to confront their flaws while also celebrating their successes.

Encourage your spouse's personal growth as an investment in your relationship. When both couples feel supported and empowered to pursue their passions, their marriage gains meaning and purpose. This shared sense of growth and accomplishment strengthens the bond, creating a dynamic and vibrant connection in which both parties may thrive.

Here are some practical strategies to encourage and support one other's personal growth and development:

- Share your aims and desires transparently and honestly. Express your hopes, concerns, feelings, and interests. Listen to your spouse's dreams and offer encouragement and support.

- Celebrate each other's accomplishments, big and small. Recognize their efforts, appreciate their victories, and express your satisfaction with their progress.

- Offer practical assistance and support. Help them overcome obstacles, develop solutions, and connect with resources that will help them achieve their goals.

- Create a space for personal development. Encourage your partner to pursue their hobbies, interests, and educational objectives. Offer to take on additional chores to free up their time.

- Show patience and understanding. Personal development involves time and effort. Be patient as your spouse improves and offer encouragement along the way.

- Respect each other's originality. Recognize that your spouse's objectives and goals may differ from your own. Encourage and celebrate their originality.

- Pray for each other's development and success. Ask God to guide and empower your spouse in their undertakings.

- Offer encouragement and motivation. Remind your spouse about their abilities, skills, and potential. Believe in them, even if they question themselves.

Supporting one another's aims should not involve pressuring your partner to reach your own goals or expectations. It's all about creating a safe and supportive environment in which they can explore their interests, pursue their own goals, and become the best versions of themselves.

When you prioritize mutual support in your marriage, you create a dynamic synergy in which both partners are motivated to grow and prosper. This mutual progress develops and deepens the tie, resulting in a more fulfilling and active partnership.

Supporting one another's aspirations is about more than just achieving individual goals; it's about leaving a lasting legacy that illustrates the power of love, encouragement, and support. It is about creating a marriage in which both partners feel respected, valued, and empowered to fulfill their lives to the fullest.

Key Points

- Shared goals and desires are essential for building a successful future together in marriage.

- Creating a shared vision includes open communication, identifying shared values and priorities, and matching individual objectives with a common aim.

- Supporting each other's personal goals and desires enhances the partnership and allows both partners to thrive.

- Regularly reviewing and refining your shared vision will help you stay on track and adjust to changing circumstances.

- Mutual support and encouragement create an environment in which both partners feel empowered to develop and achieve their full potential.

Self-Reflection Questions

1. Have you and your spouse discussed your personal and shared goals and ambitions for the future? What are some of your common goals?

____

____

____

____

____

2. How well do you support your spouse in pursuing their own goals and dreams? What more ways can you provide encouragement and practical assistance?

____

____

____

____

3. Do you feel supported by your partner to pursue your own goals and dreams? How can you better communicate your wants and desires?

____

____

____

____

4. How do your shared goals and ambitions reflect your religious beliefs and values as a couple? How do you ensure that your ambitions are consistent with God's purpose for your lives?

____

____

____

____

5. How often do you review and analyze your shared vision for the future? Are you adapting your goals and techniques as your circumstances change and you evolve as individuals?

____

____

Chapter 8: Finances: A Unified Approach

"Honor the Lord with your wealth, with the firstfruits of all your crops; then your barns will be filled to overflowing, and your vats will brim over with new wine." - Proverbs 3:9-10

Marriage finances encompass more than just spreadsheet data and bank account activities. They symbolize shared values, priorities, and dreams. They are the resources that propel your existence together, the foundation for a future built on common goals and desires.

In a Christian marriage, finances have a spiritual dimension. They become a matter of stewardship, acknowledging that all we have comes from God and is given to us for His purposes. When couples manage their finances jointly, they recognize God's ownership and work to manage their resources in ways that honor Him and reflect His standards of generosity, prudence, and responsibility.

A unified approach to finances is about more than just avoiding conflict and achieving financial stability; it's about cultivating a partnership in which both spouses feel respected, heard, and empowered to make financial choices. It is about instilling trust, transparency, and a shared sense of responsibility for managing the resources that God has entrusted to you.

Open and honest communication is vital for a unified financial strategy. It is about creating a safe space where both parties may express their financial thoughts, feelings, and concerns without fear of being judged or criticized. It entails being upfront about your income, expenses, debts, and financial objectives.

When couples discuss finances openly, they build a foundation of trust and respect. They prevent misunderstandings, hidden intentions, and financial secrets that could strain the relationship. They build a partnership in which both spouses feel involved and capable of making financial decisions.

Creating a budget together is a vital step towards financial harmony. A budget is more than just a tool for tracking income and expenses; it's a road map for achieving your financial goals, a plan for allocating your resources in a way that aligns with your values and priorities.

When couples create a budget together, they make intentional decisions about how to spend, save, and give their money. They identify areas where they can reduce expenses, increase savings, and make progress toward their financial goals. They also promote accountability and shared responsibility for financial management.

Financial goals are the compass that guides your financial journey. They provide advice, drive, and a sense of purpose in your financial decisions. When couples establish financial goals together, they create a shared vision for the future, a road map for achieving financial stability and fulfilling their dreams.

Financial goals can range from short-term objectives, such as debt repayment or saving for a down payment on a property, to long-term goals, such as retirement planning or leaving a bequest for future generations. The objective is to identify goals that are meaningful to both of you and devise a strategy for achieving them together.

Saving and investing are essential components of any successful financial plan. Saving provides a safety net for unexpected expenses and allows you to meet short-term goals, whilst investing allows you to build wealth over time and achieve your financial objectives.

Couples who save and invest together have a sense of shared ownership and responsibility for their financial future. They make decisions that are consistent with their values and goals, such as investing in companies that share their ethical beliefs or supporting causes that are important to them.

Giving is a fundamental component of a Christian financial philosophy. It recognizes that all we have is from God and was given to us for His purposes. Couples who generously donate to their church, charity organizations, and those in need put their faith into action and express gratitude to God for His provision.

Giving is more than just making monetary contributions; it is also about contributing your time, talents, and resources to assist others and make a difference in the world. Couples who donate together experience a shared sense of purpose and fulfillment, which improves their bond and enriches their relationship with God.

Managing debt is an essential component of financial responsibility. Debt may put a major strain on a marriage, producing stress, conflict, and financial instability. Couples who work together to manage and eliminate debt feel more independent and empowered, which frees up resources to pursue their goals and live a more fulfilling life.

Setting up a debt management plan comprises identifying your debts, creating a budget that prioritizes debt payments, and investigating strategies to reduce costs and enhance earnings. It may also require seeking professional guidance from a financial planner or credit counselor.

Financial unity is more than just avoiding conflict and achieving financial stability; it is about building a partnership in which both spouses feel valued, heard, and empowered to make financial decisions. It is about instilling trust, transparency, and a shared sense of responsibility for managing the resources that God has entrusted to you.

When couples deal with their finances jointly, they establish a firm foundation for their marriage based on trust and mutual respect, which will carry them through life's hardships and triumphs. They also leave a legacy of generosity, wisdom, and responsibility by showing God's love and provision via their financial choices and commitment to working together to build an honorable future.

Budgeting and Financial Planning

Money is essential in the delicate dance of marriage, where two people's lives and objectives intersect, acting as both a foundation and a road map for the journey ahead. Budgeting and financial planning, when done collectively, become not only a necessary obligation but also a powerful tool for developing a bond and establishing a safe and satisfying future together.

Making a budget as a team is not about limiting or starving yourself; it is about making conscious decisions about how you will use your resources to achieve your shared goals and objectives. It is about taking control of your finances rather than letting them dominate you. It is about creating a plan that aligns with your views, priorities, and future ambitions.

The first step in creating a budget is to document your income and expenses. This requires gathering all of your financial information, including pay stubs, bank statements, credit card statements, and any other relevant papers. It is vital to be thorough and honest during this process to ensure that you have a complete view of your financial situation.

Once you have a good understanding of your income and expenses, you can begin classifying your spending. This might help you determine where you're overspending and where you can cut back. Housing, transportation, food, utilities, entertainment, and personal care are some of the most popular spending categories.

The next stage is to set financial goals. These goals can be either short-term, such as paying off debt or saving for a down payment on a house, or long-term, such as retirement planning or funding your children's school. The objective is to identify goals that are meaningful to both of you and devise a strategy for achieving them together.

You can begin building your budget once you have determined your income, expenses, and goals. This includes dividing your money into distinct spending categories, prioritizing necessary expenses, and setting savings goals. It is vital to be realistic while budgeting to ensure that your approach is both sustainable and adaptable.

There are several budgeting systems available; choose the one that works best for you as a couple. The envelope system, the 50/30/20 budget, and zero-based budgeting are some of the most popular systems. The trick is to discover a system you can grasp and stick to.

Couples who manage their finances together must talk openly, be transparent, and be willing to collaborate. It is vital to have regular financial conversations, which include analyzing your budget, tracking your progress, and making any modifications.

Here are a few techniques to make sound financial decisions together:

- Set clear expectations and limitations. Discuss your financial values and priorities. Set clear spending and savings limits.

- Make decisions together. Do not make significant financial decisions without consulting your spouse. Collaborate to create a plan that meets both your needs and desires.

- Maintain accountability to one another. Hold each other accountable for adhering to the budget and making sound financial decisions.

- Seek expert advice if necessary. If you are experiencing financial issues or need help developing a financial plan, don't be hesitant to seek advice from a financial expert or counselor.

- Pray for wisdom and guidance. Ask God to help you manage your money wisely and make decisions that will glorify Him.

Common financial concerns in marriage can include:

- Different spending habits. One partner may spend, while the other saves.
- Debt accumulation. Credit card debt, student loans, and medical expenses can all put strain on a marriage.
- Unexpected costs. Job loss, illness, and home repairs can all hurt your finances.
- Financial infidelity. Hiding expenses or debts from your spouse can erode trust.

To address these issues, it is vital that:

- Talk openly and honestly about your financial concerns.
- Create a budget that works for both of you.
- Seek expert assistance if necessary.
- Pray for guidance and strength.

Budgeting and financial planning are more than just numbers and spreadsheets; they are about setting the groundwork for a strong marriage based on trust, mutual respect, and shared responsibility. When you approach finances collaboratively, you create a sense of security, stability, and flexibility to pursue your goals together.

Generosity and Giving

Generosity in Christian marriage includes more than just sending a cheque or donating old clothing. It is a heartfelt attitude, an open-handed mentality resulting from a deep appreciation of God's grace and bountiful supply. It's acknowledging that everything we have comes from Him and being willing to use those resources to bless others and build His kingdom.

When a couple prioritizes generosity in their marriage, they create a ripple effect of love and compassion that extends far beyond their own house. They become conduits for God's blessings, using their time, talents, and resources to make a difference in their community and around the world.

Giving is an outward expression of a generous nature. It is the act of sharing what you have, whether it is your time, talents, money, or assets. It's a practical way to demonstrate your love for God and commitment to His values of compassion, fairness, and kindness.

In a Christian marriage, gifting has a greater significance. It becomes an act of worship, a way to celebrate God with your resources while also thanking Him for His blessing. It recognizes that you are stewards of God's blessings, with the responsibility to use them wisely and for His purposes.

Giving as a couple strengthens your relationship and promotes a shared sense of purpose. It allows you to align your values and priorities while striving for the common goal of making a difference in the world. It also allows you to experience the joy of giving, which comes from using your resources to help others and build God's kingdom.

Couples can contribute to their community in a variety of ways, including by supporting organizations they care about. Here are a few ideas to inspire you.

Financial Giving:

- Tithe to your church or place of worship.
- Support missionaries and ministries that share your values.
- Donate to charities that address issues you care about, such as poverty, hunger, education, or healthcare.
- Sponsor a child or family in need.
- Join a crowdfunding campaign for a worthy cause.

Volunteering:

- Volunteer at a local soup kitchen or homeless shelter.
- Volunteer at a hospital or nursing home.
- Tutor or mentor students and young people.
- Participate in community clean-up and beautification programs.
- Offer your skills and talents to a non-profit organization.

Acts of kindness:

- Pay someone for their coffee or groceries.

- Assist an elderly neighbor with yard work or errands.
- Donate blood or platelets.
- Offer a listening ear or a helping hand to someone in need.
- Send encouraging words or letters to folks who are struggling.

Share your talents:

- Use your musical abilities to lead worship or perform at a charity event.
- Use your artistic skills to create artwork for a charity auction or fundraiser.
- Utilize your writing skills to create content for a non-profit organization or website.
- Use your teaching abilities to lead a Bible study or Sunday school class.
- Join a charitable organization's board or committee to put your leadership abilities to work.

Giving is more than just the amount donated; it is also about the motivation behind the giving. It is about giving willingly, sacrificially, and with a genuine desire to make a difference. It's about realizing that every act of giving, no matter how small, can have a ripple effect of love and compassion that extends far beyond your circle of influence.

When couples prioritize generosity and giving in their marriages, they create a legacy of love, compassion, and service. They put their faith into action by demonstrating God's love and provision in their own lives. They also develop and deepen their relationship with God by instilling a common sense of purpose and fulfillment.

Giving is a pleasure and a delight, not just a duty or obligation. It's an opportunity to join God in His purpose of redemption and restoration, to serve as His hands and feet in a world that desperately needs His love and compassion. When couples contribute together, they reap the fullness of God's blessings, not just in their own lives, but also in the lives of those they touch through their giving.

Key Points

- Finances in a Christian marriage are about stewardship, which recognizes that all resources originate from God.

- A unified financial approach requires open communication, transparency, and collaborative decision-making.

- Creating a budget together enables couples to align their spending with their values and achieve their financial objectives.

- Giving generously expresses confidence and gratitude for God's providence.

- Effective debt management is crucial for financial security and freedom.

Self-Reflection Questions

1. How do you and your partner now make financial decisions? Do you communicate clearly and openly about financial matters?

____

____

____

____

____

2. Do you share a budget? If so, how well do your marriage's values and priorities align?

____

____

____

____

____

3. How do you incorporate giving into your financial plan? Do you financially and joyfully support your church and other organizations that you believe in?

4. How well do you manage debt as a couple? Are you taking steps to get out of debt and attain financial independence?

5. What specific measures can you take to create a more coherent approach to finances in your marriage?

Chapter 9: Family and Friends

"Therefore a man shall leave his father and his mother and hold fast to his wife, and they shall become one flesh." - Genesis 2:24

Marriage, at its essence, is the creation of a new family unit, a sacred bond between two individuals who consent to live together. While love and connection between husband and wife are at the heart of this new family, extended family and friends can have a significant impact on the dynamics and health of the relationship.

In a Christian marriage, navigating these external connections has spiritual significance. It is about realizing the importance of loving and respecting family and friends but also emphasizing the marriage bond and establishing appropriate boundaries. It's about seeking God's wisdom and guidance as you navigate the complexity of these relationships, aiming to establish a healthy balance between your marriage and other important connections.

Setting proper boundaries with family and friends is crucial for preserving your marriage and building a strong foundation for your relationship. Boundaries are not barriers that keep people out; rather, they serve as guidelines for respectful and healthy interactions. They are the walls that protect your marital garden, allowing your love to flourish without being crushed by external pressures.

Establishing limits requires an open and honest talk with your spouse, family, and friends. It is important to clearly define your expectations, set boundaries for what you are comfortable with, and communicate those boundaries assertively and respectfully. It's also about having the confidence to say "no" when necessary, even if it means disappointing others.

Boundaries are not fixed, and they may need to be adjusted as your circumstances and relationship change. It is vital to examine your boundaries regularly, consult with your spouse, and make any required changes. This ongoing conversation ensures that your boundaries are healthy and useful to your marriage.

Navigating different expectations and points of view is one of the most difficult aspects of setting boundaries with loved ones. It is natural for loved ones to have perspectives on your marriage, actions, and lifestyle. However, keep in mind that your marriage is yours, and whatever decisions you make are ultimately up to you and your partner.

When presented with unsolicited counsel or criticism, respond with decency and determination. Thank them for their concern, but emphasize that this is your marriage and that you and your husband will make decisions together. It is also critical to avoid engaging in conflicts or debates that could undermine your relationships.

Another challenge is balancing the needs and desires of extended family and friends with those of your spouse. Maintaining healthy relationships with your loved ones is important, but so is prioritizing your marriage and preserving your time and energy together.

This may demand limiting how frequently you visit or spend time with family and friends. It may also mean saying "no" to requests or invitations that contradict your common priorities. The goal is to establish a balance that honors both your marriage and other important connections.

Nurturing supportive relationships outside of marriage may also serve to strengthen your bond as a couple. Surrounding yourself with friends and family who support your relationship and share your values can help you feel encouraged, guided, and a feeling of belonging.

When facing marital troubles, these supportive relationships can serve as a sounding board, offering advice and insight. They can also give you a sense of belonging and connection, reminding you that you are not alone on your path.

When choosing friends and relatives to include in your inner circle, look for those who:

- Respect your marriage. They cherish your commitment to your spouse and avoid behaviors that may endanger your relationship.

- Share your values. They have comparable views and principles, which lays the framework for mutual understanding and support.

- Offer encouragement and support. They are there for you in both good and bad times, lending a listening ear, a helping hand, and words of encouragement.

- Push yourself to improve. They motivate you to be better people and achieve success in your relationships and personal lives.

- Pray for you and your marriage. They pray for you, asking God to guide and bless your relationship.

Developing these beneficial partnerships requires effort and intention. Make time for regular communication, whether through the phone, video chat, or in-person visits. Share your joys and sorrows, offer support and encouragement, and pray for one another.

Setting proper limits and building supportive relationships are essential for a healthy and happy marriage. When you highlight your marriage bond and surround yourself with people who support it, you lay the groundwork for love, connection, and mutual respect that will carry you through life's challenges and joys.

Remember that your marriage is an individual journey, a personal agreement between you and your partner. While family and friends are important in your life, you must prioritize your relationship and create an environment in which your love may bloom without interference from others.

Setting proper limits, communicating freely and honestly, and cultivating supportive relationships will help you build a robust and vibrant marriage that honors and reflects God's love. You can leave a lasting legacy of connection, commitment, and mutual respect for future generations.

Building Healthy Boundaries

Marriage, in its most basic form, is the creation of a holy space, a shelter where two people can join together to develop a life based on love, trust, and mutual respect. While the relationship between husband and wife is central to this sanctuary, external interactions, particularly those with family and friends, can have a significant impact on the health and harmony that resides within its walls.

Building solid boundaries with family and friends does not suggest excluding or dividing them; rather, it entails defining clear rules for courteous relationships while also keeping the purity of your marriage. It's about accepting that your connection with your partner is unique and requires a level of priority that allows it to thrive in the absence of undue influence or interference.

Consider limitations to be the fences that encircle your marital garden, allowing your love to thrive and grow free of external pressures or expectations. They establish the boundaries of strong partnerships, ensuring that your relationship with your spouse remains the primary emphasis, the unshakeable foundation upon which your life together is built.

To set boundaries, communicate openly and honestly with your partner, as well as your family and friends. It is important to clearly define your expectations, set boundaries for what you are comfortable with, and communicate those boundaries assertively and respectfully. It is also critical to be able to say "no" when necessary, even if it means disappointing others or confronting opposition.

Recognizing that your marriage is your own is a vital step toward setting limits. While comments and ideas from loved ones can be useful, you and your spouse are responsible for making the final decisions about your life together. Establishing a united front, presenting yourselves as a team, and emphasizing firmly that you will make decisions together based on your common views and aspirations is vital.

When presented with unsolicited counsel or criticism, respond with decency and determination. Thank them for their concern, but underscore that your marriage is your domain, and you and your husband will chart your way together. Avoid getting involved in conflicts or debates that could strain relationships or create unnecessary stress.

Maintaining a healthy balance between your marriage and other relationships requires intentionality and wisdom. While loving and respecting your family and friends is crucial, you must also prioritize your marriage and protect your time and energy as a couple. This could include restricting how often you see or spend time with people, respectfully accepting invitations that conflict with your partnership priorities, or gently redirecting conversations that become intrusive.

Remember that limits are not fixed; they may need to be adjusted as your situation and relationship evolve. Regularly assess your limitations with your spouse, discussing any concerns or obstacles that have arisen and making modifications as needed. This ongoing conversation ensures that your boundaries are healthy and supportive of your marriage, allowing your love to flourish freely.

Navigating potentially unpleasant relationships with family or friends can be particularly challenging. If you encounter resistance or pushback while creating boundaries, remember to approach the situation with kindness, compassion, and understanding. Communicate your needs and expectations clearly, emphasizing that you do not want to create distance but rather protect the purity of your marriage.

In some cases, it may be necessary to limit contact or increase distance with specific persons whose behavior consistently breaches your boundaries or harms your relationship. This can be a difficult decision, but your marriage's health and well-being should take precedence.

Maintaining a healthy balance between your marriage and other relationships is an ongoing process that requires knowledge, caution, and a willingness to talk honestly. It's about recognizing the value of your relationships with family and friends while still emphasizing your sacred link with your spouse.

When you create proper boundaries and maintain a healthy balance, you lay a firm foundation for your marriage, creating a haven where your love can flourish without undue influence or interference. You also honor your spouse, your bond, and the holy commitment you made to God.

Remember that your marriage is a personal adventure, a precious dance between two souls seeking to build a life together. Prioritizing your relationship, setting appropriate boundaries, and communicating openly and honestly allows love to thrive, connection to deepen, and faith to grow.

Nurturing Supportive Relationships

Marriage, as a holy bond between two individuals, does not exist in a vacuum. It thrives in a network of relationships, a supportive community that protects and strengthens the husband-wife bond. Cultivating supportive friendships and relationships outside of your marriage is analogous to building a safety net, a web of loving links that can catch you when you fall and encourage you as you climb.

In a Christian marriage, these supportive bonds take on spiritual meaning. They provide support, accountability, and shared faith, forming a community in which you can grow together, pray for one another, and motivate one another to love and do good.

Intentionality is vital for fostering a supportive community. It is about meeting people who share your beliefs and interests, believe in the sanctity of marriage, and are committed to their spiritual development. It is about creating a setting in which you can be vulnerable, communicate your struggles and joys, and receive support and prayer.

This community can be found in a variety of settings, such as churches, small groups, Bible studies, and even online communities. The goal is to find a place where you may feel connected, encouraged, and challenged as you advance in your religion and marriage.

Here are some suggestions for building a network of support:

- Get involved in your church. Attend services regularly, participate in small groups or Bible studies, and volunteer your time and skills.

- Join a couples' group or ministry. Connect with other couples who are committed to building their marriages and growing in faith together.

- Look for mentors or older couples who can share their knowledge and wisdom. Learn from their experiences, gain insights from their journeys, and feel inspired and supported.

- Attend a marriage conference or retreat. These events provide you the opportunity to learn from experts, network with other couples, and invest in your relationship.

- Connect with other couples online. Join an online community or forum to share your experiences, ask questions, and receive support from others.

Finding mentors or role models can be quite beneficial in your marriage journey. These are people who have experienced the ups and downs of marriage, who have survived storms and emerged stronger, and who can offer advice, guidance, and encouragement to those who follow in their footsteps.

When your marriage is going through a rough patch, mentors may provide a listening ear, a shoulder to cry on, and a voice of reason. They can offer insight, share their own experiences, and provide practical advice for overcoming challenges and improving your partnership.

Role models can inspire you by exemplifying a strong and successful marriage. They can demonstrate the power of dedication, communication, and faith via action. They may demonstrate how to love and adore your spouse, prioritize your relationship, and live a life together that glorifies God.

Here are some guidelines for identifying mentors and role models:

- Look around your church or community. Find couples with a strong and vibrant marriage who are actively committed to helping others.

- Reach out to elderly couples that you appreciate. Ask them if they would be willing to share their knowledge and experiences with you.

- Attend a marriage conference or retreat. These events usually feature speakers and individuals who serve as role models and mentors.

- Read books or listen to podcasts by Christian authors and presenters about marriage. Learn from their viewpoints and apply what you learn to your relationship.

- Pray that God will connect you with mentors and role models. Ask Him to bring people into your life who can offer counsel and support.

Nurturing positive connections requires effort and intention. Make time for regular communication, whether through the phone, video chat, or in-person visits. Share your joys and sorrows, offer support and encouragement, and pray for one another.

These relationships are not meant to replace your primary relationship with your spouse, but to supplement and improve it. They provide a network of support, encouragement, and accountability to help you navigate the challenges of marriage while also celebrating its delights.

When you prioritize building a support community and seeking mentors or role models, you create a safety net for your marriage, a network of caring links that may help you navigate life's ups and downs. You also leave a legacy of connection, commitment, and mutual support for future generations.

<u>**Key Points**</u>

- Healthy boundaries with family and friends are critical for sustaining your marriage and prioritizing your relationship.

- Open communication with your spouse and loved ones is essential for establishing and maintaining limits.

- Balancing the needs of your marriage with those of your extended family and friends requires foresight and insight.

- Surrounding oneself with supportive relationships can strengthen your marriage and develop a sense of community.

- Seeking out mentors or role models can provide guidance and support as you navigate your marriage.

<u>**Self-Reflection Questions**</u>

1. What boundaries have you established with family and friends to protect your marriage? Are these boundaries communicated and respected?

____

____

____

____

____

2. How do you combine the demands and expectations of your extended family and friends with your marriage? Are there any areas where you should shift your priorities?

3. Who is the most helpful person in your relationship? How do these relationships help your marriage?

4. Do you have any mentors or role models who have encouraged you in your marriage journey? How can you obtain more advice and assistance from those who have already taken this path?

5. How can you strengthen your marriage's support network within your church and beyond?

Chapter 10: Serving Together

"Each of you should use whatever gift you have received to serve others, as faithful stewards of God's grace in its various forms." - 1 Peter 4:10

Marriage, in its most basic form, is a relationship between two people who agree to share their lives. However, it is also an outward-facing entity, a unit that interacts with the outside world, contributing to the greater good and having a constructive impact on society. When couples serve together, they not only enhance their relationship but also practice their faith in practical ways, reflecting God's love and compassion on others around them.

Serving together is like adding a new layer to your marriage: a common purpose that transcends your individual needs and goals. It is about looking beyond yourself recognizing the needs of others, and then using your time, abilities, and resources to make a difference in the world. This shared commitment to service creates a sense of belonging and purpose, which strengthens and deepens your friendship.

Serving in a Christian marriage has spiritual significance. It becomes an act of worship, a way to exalt God with your offerings while also praising Him for His abundance. It recognizes that your talents and abilities are not only for your benefit but also for the good of others and the growth of His kingdom.

When couples serve together, they create a ripple effect of love and compassion that extends far beyond their own homes. They become change agents, beacons of hope, and reflections of God's grace in a world that yearns for His presence. This shared commitment to service not only strengthens their marriage but also inspires others to follow in their footsteps, sparking a chain reaction of kindness and generosity.

Finding shared ministry opportunities is a fantastic way to combine your interests and abilities while helping others. It is about recognizing areas where your unique skills complement one another, resulting in synergistic cooperation in which you may do more together than you could alone.

Perhaps one spouse is passionate about teaching while the other is talented in music. They could collaborate to lead a children's ministry or a worship group. Perhaps one spouse loves working with the elderly, whereas the other is passionate about assisting the homeless. They could volunteer at a local soup kitchen or nursing home.

The alternatives are unlimited. The goal is to find areas where your passions and talents cross, resulting in a collaborative ministry that brings you joy and fulfillment. This common aim will not only strengthen your connection as a couple, but it will also enable you to make a significant difference in the lives of others.

Making an influence in your community doesn't require grand gestures or heroic efforts. It can be as simple as offering assistance to a neighbor, volunteering at a local school, or donating to a nonprofit organization. The idea is to be intentional in seeking out opportunities to serve and positively impact the world around you.

Here are a few ideas to inspire you.

- Volunteer for a local charity or non-profit organization. Volunteer your time and skills to help a cause you care about, such as assisting the homeless, feeding the hungry, or assisting those in need.

- Get involved in your church or community. Participate in outreach efforts, volunteer for leadership positions, or apply your skills and talents to benefit your community.

- Mentor or tutor young people. Share your expertise, experience, and wisdom to guide and inspire future generations.

- Please support your local businesses and organizations. Support businesses that reflect your values, donate to local charities and take part in community events.

- Be a good neighbor. Help those around you, whether by mowing an elderly neighbor's lawn, preparing a dinner for a new parent, or just listening.

Serving as a couple is more than just doing good; it is demonstrating God's love and compassion to others around you. It is about being His hands and feet in a world that desperately requires His presence. When you serve together, you not only strengthen your bond but also become a source of hope and inspiration to others.

Serving together can be a powerful tool for personal and spiritual growth. It may encourage you to step beyond your comfort zone, face your own biases and prejudices, and build greater understanding and compassion for others. It might also enhance your faith as you witness God's work in the lives of individuals you support.

When couples collaborate, they create an enduring legacy of love, compassion, and service. They demonstrate their commitment to each other, the community, and their ideals. They build a strong foundation for their marriage on shared values and mutual purpose, which will carry them through life's challenges and joys.

Serving together is not just a duty or an obligation; it is a privilege and a pleasure. It's an opportunity to join God in His purpose of redemption and restoration, to serve as His hands and feet in a world that desperately needs His love and compassion. Couples who serve together reap the fullness of God's benefits, not only in their own lives but also in the lives of those they touch via service.

Finding Shared Ministry Opportunities

Serving in ministry as a couple is like adding vibrant color to your marriage's canvas, a shared experience that deepens your connection strengthens your bond, and allows your love to light out into the world. It recognizes that your partnership is about more than just your happiness and fulfillment; it is also about helping others and making a difference in your community and beyond.

When couples agree to collaborate, they create a unique synergy, a powerful force for good that doubles their efforts and broadens their impact. They constitute a team, working toward a common goal, complementing one another's strengths, and motivating one another through challenges.

This common commitment to service benefits not just the people they help, but also serves as the foundation for their cooperation. It improves mutual understanding, allows for shared experiences, and enhances their spiritual and emotional bonds. It reflects their shared views, commitment to their faith, and desire to make a difference in our world.

Serving together also allows couples to grow in their religious beliefs. As they step outside of their comfort zone and use their gifts and talents to help others, they experience God's love and grace in new and profound ways. They witness the transformative power of His work in the lives of those they serve, and they are reminded of His invitation to be His hands and feet in the world.

The options for serving as a couple are as diverse as the couples themselves. Each couple possesses a distinct set of qualities, talents, and passions that they can utilize to benefit others and advance God's kingdom. The objective is to identify your abilities seek out missionary opportunities that align with your interests and allow you to put your talents to the best use.

The following are some examples of numerous ministry opportunities that couples can consider:

- Children's Ministry: If you care about children, consider volunteering with your church's children's ministry. You could teach Sunday school, direct a children's choir, or help with Vacation Bible School.

- Youth Ministry: If you enjoy working with teenagers, consider volunteering for your church's youth ministry. You may lead small-group discussions, monitor youth events, or mentor young people.

- Music Ministry: If you have musical ability, consider volunteering in your church's music program. You could sing in the choir, play an instrument in the praise band, or lead worship services.

- Hospitality Ministry: If you enjoy greeting and assisting others, consider joining your church's hospitality ministry. You could greet visitors, usher at services, or help with church activities and festivities.

- Missions: If you want to help those in need, consider participating in a mission trip. You may travel to another country to build houses, provide medical care, or promote the gospel. You might also contribute locally by volunteering at a homeless shelter, soup kitchen, or community outreach program.

- Counseling or Mentoring: If you have a talent for listening and helping others, consider becoming a counselor or mentor to other couples or individuals. You might offer premarital counseling, marriage enrichment seminars, and one-on-one mentoring.

If you enjoy teaching or leading, consider taking up a leadership position in your church or community. You may lead a Bible study, form a small group, or sit on a church board or committee.

These are just a few of the many ways couples can serve together. The most important thing is to find missionary possibilities that match your interests, capabilities, and abilities. When you serve together in areas that are meaningful to both of you, you build a common sense of purpose and fulfillment, which strengthens your bond and improves your relationship with God.

Finding common ministry possibilities may need extensive investigation and deep reflection. Tell your spouse about your interests, talents, and desire to serve others. Please pray for God's wisdom and direction. Look for opportunities in your church or community that match your interests and skills.

Serving together is more than just fulfilling a chore or obligation; it demonstrates your love for God and commitment to His kingdom. It is about using your skills and abilities to benefit others and change the world. It is about strengthening your relationship as a couple and connecting with God.

When you serve together, you unleash a wave of love, compassion, and positive change that extends far beyond your own house. You become a beacon of hope, expressing the strength of faith through action. You also leave a legacy of service and generosity that will inspire others and have long-term consequences for your community and the world.

Making a Difference in Your Community

Your community, the network of people and families who surround you, is more than just a geographical location; it is a dynamic ecosystem of lives, each with its own distinct story, set of challenges, and successes. As a couple, you have the potential to be a beacon of light and hope in this atmosphere, causing a positive ripple effect that touches lives and improves the fabric of your community.

Making a difference in your community doesn't require grand gestures or heroic efforts; rather, it takes small, everyday acts of kindness, compassion, and service that have a positive ripple effect. It is about seeing the needs in your community and responding with a kind heart, volunteering your time, talents, and resources to make it a better place for everybody.

In a Christian marriage, this dedication to communal impact is especially important. It becomes an expression of faith in action, a means of carrying out Christ's teachings and displaying His love for the world. It is the realization that your marriage is for more than just your happiness and fulfillment; it is about blessing others and making a difference in the world.

When couples work together in their community, they strengthen and deepen their relationship. They share their experiences, strive for common goals, and enjoy the feeling of making a difference together. They also learn from one another, respect each other's skills, and help one another overcome their weaknesses.

Serving together is also an opportunity to enhance your religious beliefs. When you step outside of your comfort zone and use your gifts and talents to help others, you will find God's love and grace in new and significant ways. You witness the impact of His work in the lives of those you serve, and you are reminded of His invitation to be His hands and feet in the world.

Here are some helpful recommendations for taking part in local outreach efforts or volunteer opportunities:

- Contact your neighborhood church or place of worship. Many churches offer a variety of outreach and volunteer options, such as food pantries, homeless shelters, after-school programs, and community service projects. Speak with your pastor or church leaders about how to get involved.

- Investigate local non-profit organizations. Identify organizations that share your interests and values, such as those that address poverty, hunger, homelessness, education, or environmental challenges. For additional information about volunteer opportunities, please visit their websites or contact them directly.

- Volunteer in a local school or community center. Offer to teach pupils, mentor children, or assist with after-school activities. Contact the school or community center to learn about their needs and how you can help.

- Participate in community clean-up and beautification programs. Contribute to making your neighborhood a more welcoming and exciting place to live. Check with your local government or community organizations for upcoming events and activities.

- Support local businesses and organizations that are committed to giving back to their communities. Shop at local stores, dine at local restaurants, and support businesses that share your beliefs. This boosts the local economy and encourages businesses to continue their philanthropic efforts.

- Be a good neighbor. Help those in need, whether by shoveling snow, mowing the lawn, or just listening. Creating close relationships with your neighbors promotes a sense of community and support.

- Use your professional experience to assist others. Provide pro bono legal services and medical care to those in need, or use your artistic talents to bring beauty and hope. Use your abilities and knowledge to better the lives of others.

- Plan a community service project with your friends and family. Form a group to volunteer at a local charity, clean up a park, or raise money for a worthy cause. This is a fantastic way to get your loved ones involved in community service and build a shared sense of giving back.

- Use social media to raise awareness for local causes and organizations. Share volunteer opportunities, donate to online fundraisers, and encourage others to participate. Use your online platform to advocate for those in need and promote positive change.

Making an impact in your community takes more than just donating your time and money; it also entails building relationships, connecting with your neighbors, and establishing a sense of belonging. It is about becoming a light in the darkness, spreading God's love and compassion to those around you.

Here are some alternative ways to have a great effect in your community:

- Practice random acts of kindness. Pay for someone's coffee, congratulate a stranger, or write a meaningful letter to a neighbor. These small gestures can brighten someone's day and create a positive ripple effect.

- Be a good listener. Offer a listening ear to those who are struggling or going through a difficult time. Sometimes the most valuable gift you can give is your time and attention.

- Show compassion and empathy. Seek to understand the perspectives and experiences of others, including those who differ from you. This improves understanding and creates a more inclusive community.

- Stand up for justice and equality. Speak up against injustice and discrimination, and help those who are marginalized or oppressed. Use your voice to promote fairness and equality for everyone.

- Be a peacemaker. Seek to handle problems amicably and promote understanding and healing in your community. Be a bridge builder and contribute to a more peaceful environment.

- Live a life of integrity. Be truthful, trustworthy, and accountable in your interactions with others. Your actions speak louder than your words, and living ethically fosters trust and respect.

- Share your religion with others. Your words and actions will provide witness to God's love and grace. Allow your light to shine brightly throughout your community, illuminating God's love for everyone around you.

Making a difference in your community requires a lifetime dedication to service and compassion. It's about understanding that you're a part of something larger than yourself and that your actions, no matter how small, can have far-reaching implications.

When couples volunteer in their community, they not only help others but also strengthen their bond and improve their relationship with God. They enjoy giving, are fulfilled by using their strengths and talents to assist others, and are satisfied knowing that they are making a difference in the world.

Key Points

- Serving as a couple fosters camaraderie, strengthens your connection with God, and has a positive impact on your community.

- Discovering shared ministry opportunities allows you to use your skills and talents to help others and build God's kingdom together.

- Making an impact in your community can be accomplished through volunteering, participating in outreach programs, supporting local organizations, and performing everyday acts of kindness.

- Serving together provides opportunities for personal and spiritual growth as you step outside of your comfort zones and see God's love in action.

- Living a life of service reflects your values and objectives, leaving a mark of love and compassion in your community.

Self-Reflection Questions

1. How do you and your spouse actively participate in your community? What are some areas where you could increase your involvement?

____

____

____

____

2. What are your shared passions and interests? How can you combine your interests to best benefit others?

____

____

____

____

3. What gifts and talents do you each possess? How can you use your abilities to create a greater impact in your community?

____

____

____

____

____

4. Which local organizations or causes do you feel drawn to support? How can you contribute and make a difference?

____

____

____

____

____

5. How has serving together impacted your marriage and personal relationship with God?

____

____

____

____

____

Conclusion

As we come to the end of this workbook, let us reflect on our journey together. We've looked into the power of prayer, learned from God's Word, and discovered ways to speak openly and honestly. We've practiced settling arguments, recognizing each other's love languages, and developing closeness at all levels. We've considered our future, devised a financial strategy, and discovered methods to build a supportive community around our marriage.

This workbook has been a valuable resource as we seek to strengthen our marriage and deepen our faith. The real work comes now, as we apply what we've learned to our daily lives.

Remember that creating a strong and fulfilling Christian marriage is a lifetime journey. It takes commitment, effort, and a willingness to grow, both individually and as a partnership. It's about making daily decisions to prioritize our connection, to be open and honest with one another, to forgive freely, and to seek God's presence in all situations.

As we continue on this route, let's remember these key principles:

- Prayer is the basis of our marriage. Make prayer a regular component of our lives, both collectively and individually. Seek God's direction and strength in all situations.

- God's Word is our guidance. Study the Bible together and allow its truths to affect our thinking and actions.

- Communication is crucial. Be open and honest with one another, and listen to understand.

- Disagreements might result in growth. Learn how to settle conflict healthily, find understanding, and achieve peace.

- Show love in ways that our partner understands. Learn each other's love languages and show your adoration in meaningful ways.

- Intimacy is more than just physical. Encourage emotional, spiritual, and intellectual connections as well.

- Look to the future together. Create a shared vision for our lives, encourage one another's dreams, and work together to achieve common goals.

- Handle our finances wisely. Be transparent about money and use our resources appropriately.

- Choose our partnerships wisely. Set good boundaries with family and friends, and look for people that support our marriage.

- Serve others together. Find ways to use our gifts to benefit our community while also growing in our faith.

As you apply these ideas, you will discover that your marriage becomes a source of strength, joy, and fulfillment. You'll form a strong bond that can resist hardships, a love that deepens over time, and a partnership that praises God.

Remember, you are not alone on this journey. God is constantly with you, providing guidance and strength. Rely on Him, believe in His promises, and let Him work in your life and marriage.

Your marriage is a valuable gift, a sacred promise bestowed by God. On a daily basis, cherish, nurture, and invest. As you do, your love story will serve as a monument to God's love's ability to unite, heal, and create long-lasting joy.

May your marriage shine a light on others, reflect Christ's love, and bring blessings to all those around us.

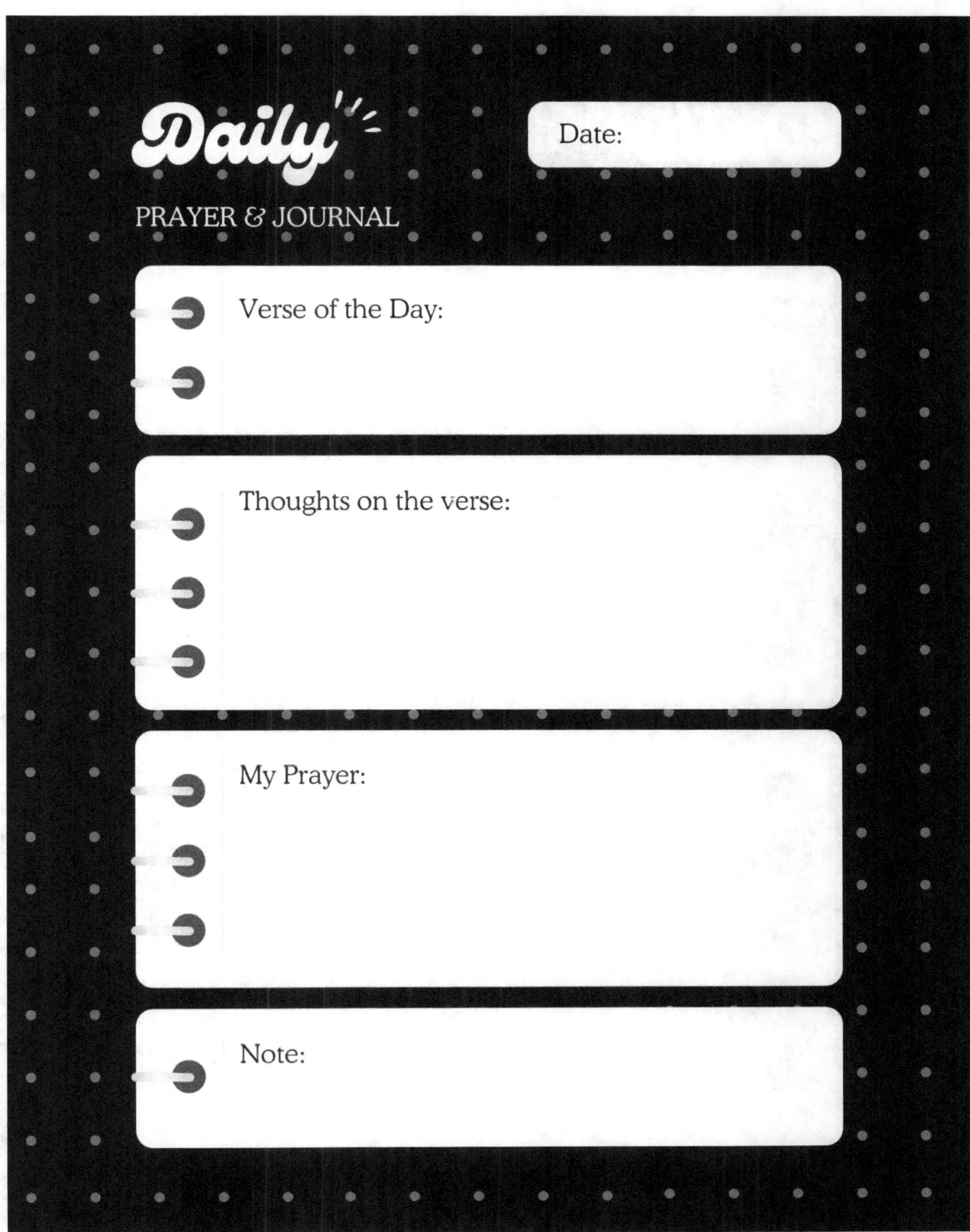

Daily
PRAYER & JOURNAL
Date:
Verse of the Day:
Thoughts on the verse:
My Prayer:
Note:

Daily

PRAYER & JOURNAL

Date:

Verse of the Day:

Thoughts on the verse:

My Prayer:

Note:

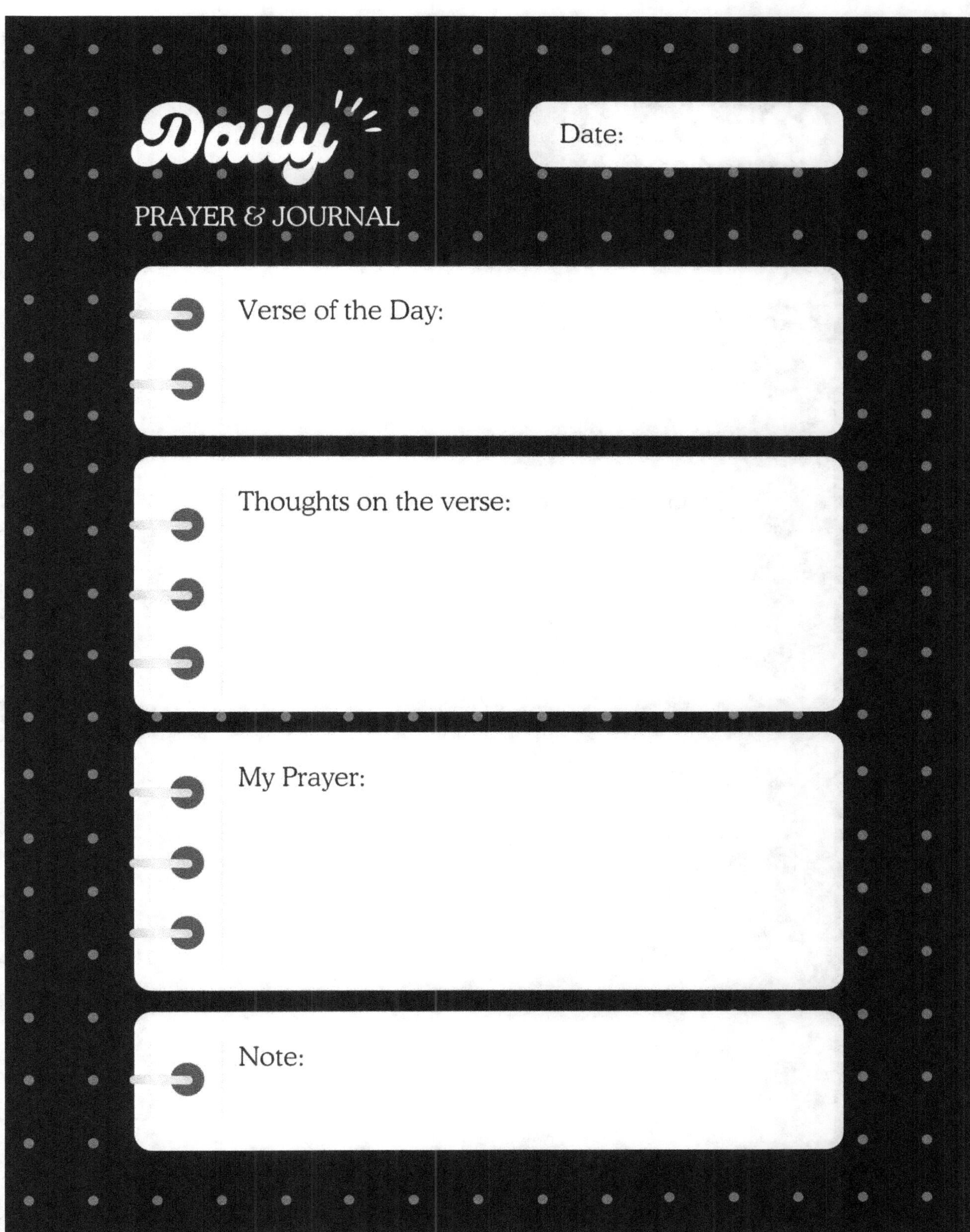

Daily
PRAYER & JOURNAL
Date:
Verse of the Day:
Thoughts on the verse:
My Prayer:
Note:

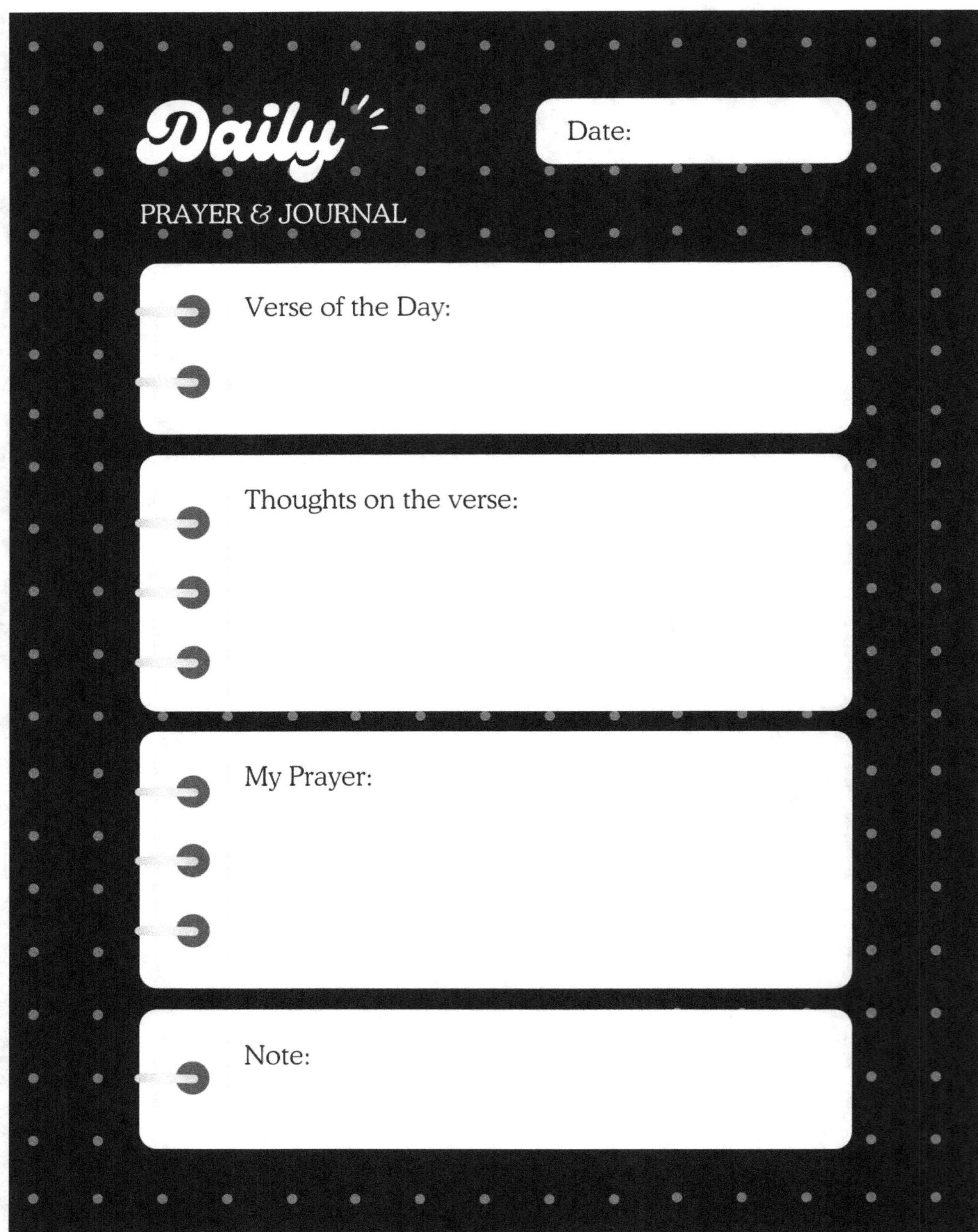

Daily
PRAYER & JOURNAL
Date:
Verse of the Day:
Thoughts on the verse:
My Prayer:
Note:

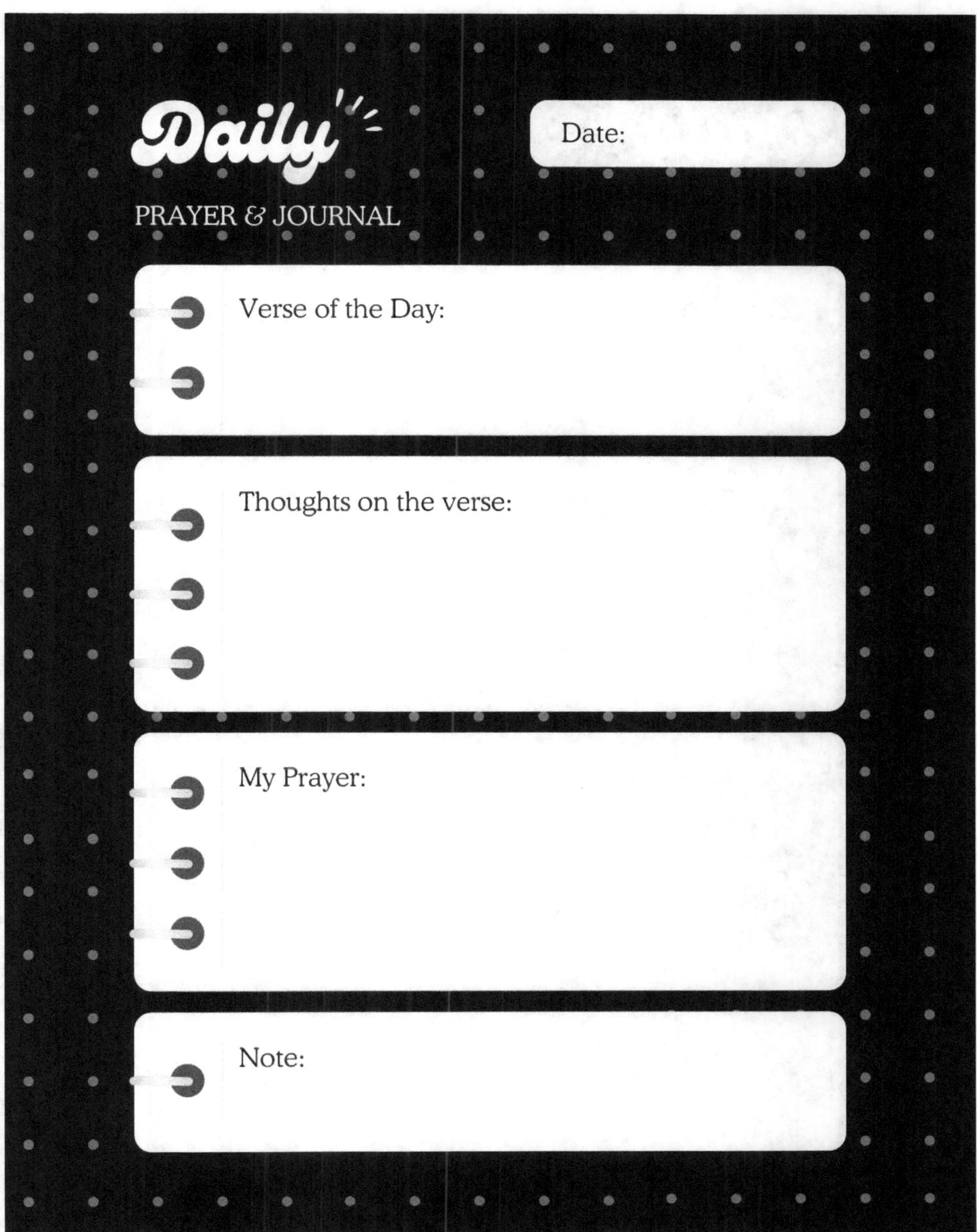

Daily
PRAYER & JOURNAL
Date:
Verse of the Day:
Thoughts on the verse:
My Prayer:
Note:

Daily

PRAYER & JOURNAL

Date:

Verse of the Day:

Thoughts on the verse:

My Prayer:

Note:

Daily
PRAYER & JOURNAL
Date:
Verse of the Day:
Thoughts on the verse:
My Prayer:
Note:

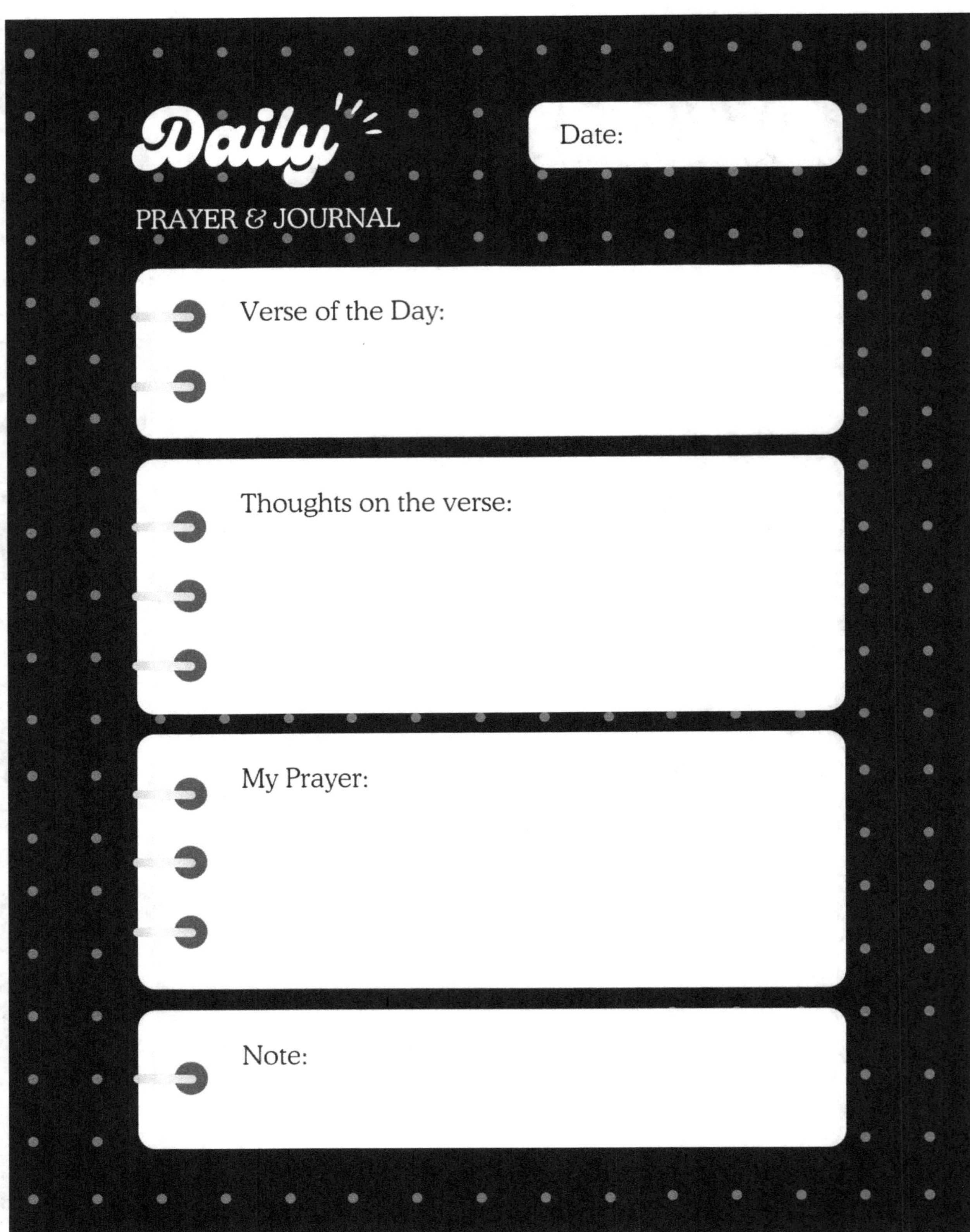
Daily
PRAYER & JOURNAL
Date:
Verse of the Day:
Thoughts on the verse:
My Prayer:
Note:

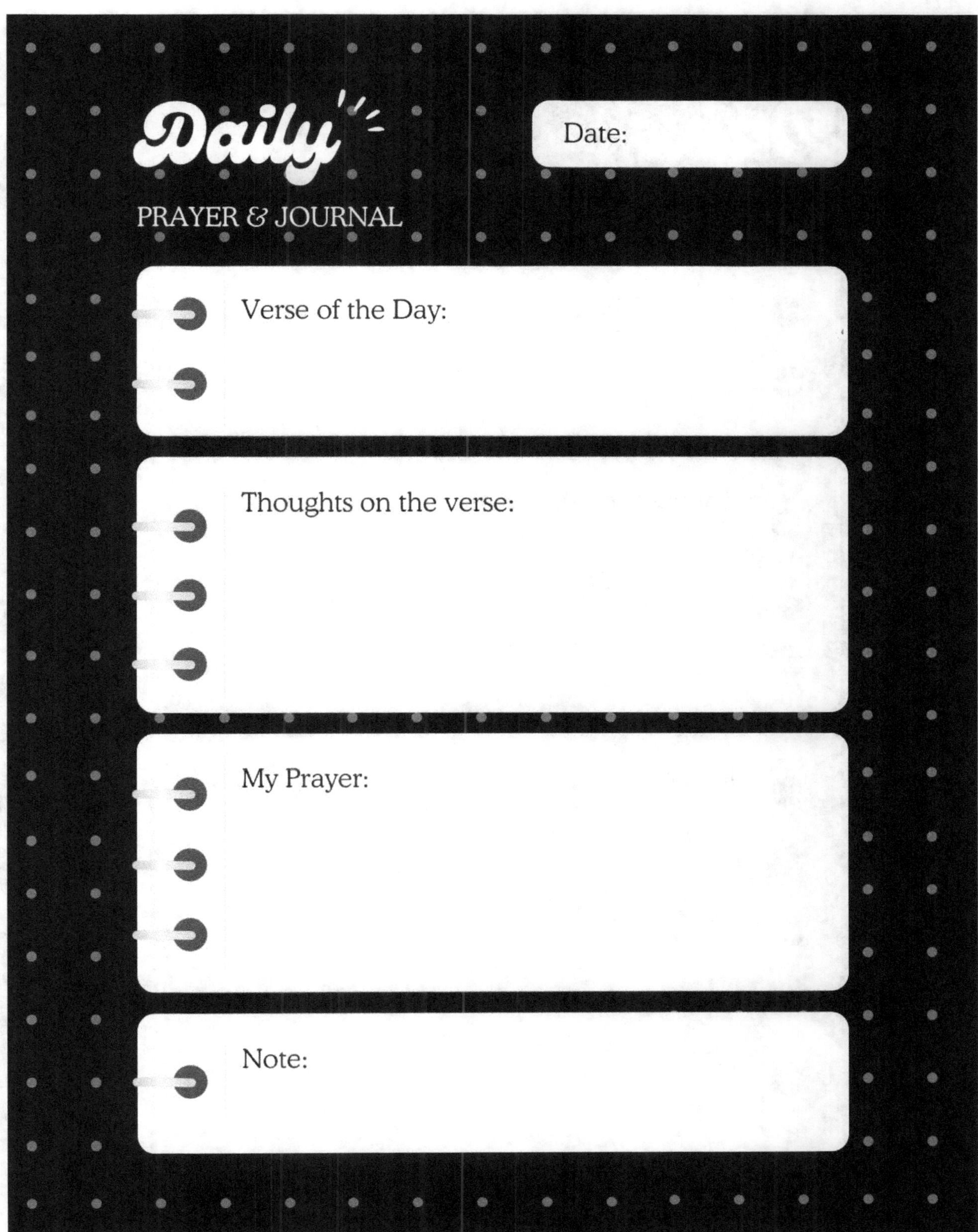

Daily
PRAYER & JOURNAL
Date:
Verse of the Day:
Thoughts on the verse:
My Prayer:
Note:

Daily

PRAYER & JOURNAL

Date:

Verse of the Day:

Thoughts on the verse:

My Prayer:

Note: